WHEN THE GAME IS OVER

IT ALL GOES

BACK IN THE

B₃ O₁ X₈

Resources by John Ortberg

An Ordinary Day with Jesus
(curriculum series, with Ruth Haley Barton)

Everybody's Normal Till You Get to Know Them
(book, audio, curriculum)

God Is Closer Than You Think
(book, audio, curriculum with Stephen and Amanda Sorenson)

If You Want to Walk on Water, You've Got to Get Out of the Boat
(book, audio, curriculum with Stephen and Amanda Sorenson)

Know Doubt
(formerly Faith & Doubt)

The Life You've Always Wanted
(book, audio, curriculum with Stephen and Amanda Sorenson)

Living the God Life

Love Beyond Reason

The Me I Want to Be
(book, audio)

Old Testament Challenge
(curriculum series, with Kevin and Sherry Harney)

When the Game Is Over, It All Goes Back in the Box
(book, audio, curriculum with Stephen and Amanda Sorenson)

JOHN ORTBERG

Author of If You Want to Walk on Water, You've Got to Get Out of the Boat

WHEN THE GAME IS OVER

IT ALL GOES

BACK IN THE

 ZONDERVAN®

WILLOW
Willow Creek Resources

ZONDERVAN.com/
AUTHORTRACKER
follow your favorite authors

ZONDERVAN

When the Game Is Over, It All Goes Back in the Box
Copyright © 2007 by John Ortberg

This title is also available as a Zondervan ebook.
Visit www.zondervan.com/ebooks.

This title is also available in a Zondervan audio edition.
Visit www.zondervan.fm.

Requests for information should be addressed to:
Zondervan, *Grand Rapids, Michigan* 49530

This edition: ISBN 978-0-310-32505-5 (softcover)

Library of Congress Cataloging-in-Publication Data

Ortberg, John.
    When the game is over, it all goes back in the box / John Ortberg.
       p. cm.
    Includes bibliographical references.
    ISBN 978-0-310-25350-1 (hardcover)
    1. Christian life. I. Title.
  BV4501.3.0768   2007
  248.4—dc22   2007006673

Interior design: Beth Shagene

Printed in the United States of America

9 10 11 12 13 14 15 16 • 23 22 21 20 19 18 17 16 15 14 13 12 11 10 9 8 7 6 5 4 3 2

CONTENTS

HOW TO PLAY

HAZARDS

TO WIN

INTRODUCTION

Somebody a long time ago said that life is a game, and that is the main image behind this book. In using this image, I'm not saying that we should take our lives lightly. G. K. Chesterton once wrote that while we often take ourselves too seriously, we can hardly take our souls seriously enough. But life, like a game, is moving toward a goal. It has an object; it is not just a series of random activities. Furthermore, there are rules to follow in life, and each of us will develop a strategy. The game will not go on forever. As an ancient Italian proverb puts it, "Pawn and king alike, they all go back in the bag." An outcome is inevitable. (I am indebted to James Dobson for this image, from his book *Straight Talk to Men* [Sisters, OR: Multnomah, 1984], 19–20.)

How to play the game of life is what this book is about. The instructions are listed in the table of contents. Though it is best to know and play by all the rules, each chapter—each principle of the game—can be appreciated on its own and applied to the game of life. So feel free to skip around.

One of the most widely read manuscripts in the Middle Ages was an allegory that compared life to a game of chess. The anonymous author wrote, "Wherefore play the game of life warily, for your opponent is full of subtlety, and take abundant thought over your moves, for the stake is your soul."

Have a good game.

ACKNOWLEDGMENTS

One of the lessons (besides the primary message of this book) that my grandmother taught was to say thank-you, and it is a pleasure to do so to people who have helped make this book a reality. My daughter Laura devoted the better part of a summer to do research and help shape it, and she has been over each draft with a fine-tooth comb.

Although it is generally wise never to switch horses in the middle of a stream, I got to work with two unusually generous and helpful editors this time around. Jack Kuhatschek is an old friend, and John Sloan is a new one, and both of them are alarmingly creative editors. The entire team at Zondervan is a joy to partner with, as is Trudi Barnes, who works in the office right next to mine.

Also, I am deeply grateful to the congregation I serve in Menlo Park for making the time available for me to write, and to the men of integrity who meet on Saturday mornings and hold me up in prayer.

I am grateful to my father and mother and sister and brother for teaching me so much of how to play and live. So this book is lovingly dedicated to John and Kathy and Barbara and Barton.

And to Gram.

And, as always, to Nancy.

THE GAME

CHAPTER 1

LEARN RULE #1

This is our predicament.
Over and over again, we lose sight of
what is important and what isn't.
EPICTETUS

My grandmother had just gotten out of jail.

She was a roll away from the yellow properties. And the yellow properties meant trouble. They were mine. And they had hotels. And Gram had no money. She had wanted to stay in jail longer to avoid landing on my property and having to cough up dough she did not have, but she rolled doubles, and that meant her bacon was going to get fried.

I was a ten-year-old sitting at the Monopoly table. I had it all—money and property, houses and hotels, Boardwalk and Park Place. I had been a loser at this game my whole life, but today was different, as I knew it would be. Today I was Donald Trump, Bill Gates, Ivan the Terrible. Today my grandmother was one roll of the dice away from ruin. And I was one roll of the dice away from the biggest lesson life has to teach: the absolute necessity of arranging our life around what matters in light of our mortality and eternity. It is a lesson that some of the smartest people in the world forget but that my grandmother was laser clear on.

For my grandmother taught me how to play the game....

Golda Hall, my mother's mother, lived with us in the corner bedroom when I was growing up. She was a greathearted person. She was built soft and round, the way grandmothers were before they took up aerobics. She remains, at least in the memories of my boyhood, the

most purely fun person I have known. She let us stay up later than
we were supposed to on Friday nights when our parents were gone.
She peeled apples for us, told us ghost stories and scary old poems
("Little Orphan Annie came to our house to stay ...") that kept us
awake for hours. She baked banana bread that was like having dessert
for breakfast and made us red velvet cake — which consists mostly of
butter — on our birthdays.

And she taught me how to play the game.

My grandmother was a game player, and she did not like to lose.
She didn't get mean or mad, but she still (to use an expression from
her childhood world) had some snap in her girdle. It was part of her
charm. Every Friday night as long as my grandfather was alive, the
whole family, including spouses, would gather to play a card game
called Rook; and if you were Gram's partner, it was not wise to miss
a trick or lose the bid. Everyone's favorite old home movie featured
Gram playing in a softball game at a family picnic in her younger
days. She made contact with the ball and ran the bases with such
singleness of purpose — a large woman coming at you like Bronco
Nagurski — that no one got in her way. Home run. When she played
Chinese checkers with small grandchildren, she was not one of those
pushover grandmothers who would lose on purpose to make the
grandchildren feel better about themselves. Gram believed before
Max De Pree ever said it that a leader's first task is to define reality.
She was the leader, and the reality was that she played to win. Pout-
ing and self-pity, two of my spiritual gifts, did not elicit sympathy from
her, for even when she was playing, she kept an eye on what kind of
person you were becoming. And my grandmother taught me how to
play the game.

The Master of the Board

Grandmother was at her feistiest when it came to Monopoly. Periodi-
cally leaders like General Patton or Attila the Hun develop a reputation for toughness. They were lapdogs next to her. Imagine that Vince

Lombardi had produced an offspring with Lady MacBeth, and you get some idea of the competitive streak that ran in my grandmother. She was a gentle and kind soul, but at the Monopoly table she would still take you to the cleaners.

When I got the initial $1,500 from the banker to start the game, I always wanted to hang on to my money as long as possible. You never know what Chance card might turn up next. The board is a risky place. I am half Swedish (on my father's side), and Swedes are not high rollers.

"Don't worry about it," my grandmother would say. "One day you'll learn to play the game."

But my grandmother knew how to play the game. She understood that you don't win without risk, and she didn't play for second place. So she would spend every dollar she got. She would buy every piece of property she landed on. She would mortgage every piece of property she owned to the hilt in order to buy everything else.

She understood what I did not—that accumulating is the name of the game, that money is how you keep score, that the race goes to the swift. She played with skill, passion, and reckless abandon. Eventually, inevitably, she would become Master of the Board. When you're the Master of the Board, you own so much property that no one else can hurt you. When you're Master of the Board, you're in control. Other players regard you with fear and envy, shock and awe. From that point on, it's only a matter of time. She would watch me land on Boardwalk one time too many, hand over to her what was left of my money, and put my little race car marker away, all the time wondering why I had lost yet again. "Don't worry about it," she'd say. "One day you'll learn to play the game."

I hated it when she said that.

Then one year when I was ten, I spent a summer playing Monopoly every day with a kid named Steve who lived kitty-corner from me. Gradually it dawned on me that the only way to win this game was to make a total commitment to acquisition. No mercy. No fear. What my grandmother had been showing me for so long finally sank in.

By the fall, when we sat down to play, I was more ruthless than she was. My palms were sweaty. I would play without softness or caution. I was ready to bend the rules if I had to. Slowly, cunningly, I exposed the soft underbelly of my grandmother's vulnerability. Relentlessly, inexorably, I drove her off the board. (The game does strange things to you.)

I can still remember—it happened at Marvin Gardens.

I looked at my grandmother—this was the woman who had taught me how to play. She was an old lady by now. A widow. She had raised my mother. She loved my mother, as she loved me. And I took everything she had. I destroyed her financially and psychologically. I watched her give up her last dollar and quit in utter defeat.

It was the greatest moment of my life.

I had won. I was cleverer, and stronger, and more ruthless than anyone else at the table. I was Master of the Board.

But then my grandmother had one more thing to teach me. The greatest lesson comes at the end of the game. And here it is. In the words of James Dobson, who described this lesson from Monopoly in playing with his family many years ago: *"Now it all goes back in the box."*

All those houses and hotels. All that property—Boardwalk and Park Place, the railroads and the utility companies. All those thousands of dollars. *When the game is over, it all goes back in the box.*

I didn't want it to go back in the box. I wanted to leave it out as a perpetual memorial to my skill at playing the game—to bronze it, perhaps, so others could admire my tenacity and success. I wanted the sense of power that goes with being Master of the Board to last forever. I wanted the thrill of winning to be my perpetual companion. I was so heady with victory after all these years that for a few moments I lost touch with reality. None of that stuff was mine—not really. Now, for a few moments, it was my turn to play the game. I could get all steamed up about it for a while and act as if the game were going to last forever. But it would not. Not for me. Not for you either. Plato said that the entire task of philosophy can be summed up as *melete thanatou*—"mindfulness of death."

I am a Christian, and I seek to write this book from the perspective of faith. I believe that you are a ceaseless being with an eternal destiny in the universe of an unimaginably good God. But you don't even have to believe in the Bible to understand the lesson of the box. Comedian Jerry Seinfeld put it like this:

> To me, if life boils down to one significant thing, it's movement. To live is to keep moving. Unfortunately, this means that for the rest of our lives we're going to be looking for boxes.
>
> When you're moving, your whole world is boxes. That's all you think about. "Boxes, where are the boxes?" You just wander down the street going in and out of stores, "Are there boxes here? Have you seen any boxes?" It's all you think about.
>
> You could be at a funeral, everyone around you is mourning, crying, and you're looking at the casket. "That's a nice box. Does anybody know where that guy got that box? When he's done with it, you think I could get it? It's got some nice handles on it. My stereo would fit right in there."
>
> I mean that's what death is, really—the last big move of your life. The hearse is like the van, the pall bearers are your close friends, the only ones you could really ask to help you with a big move like that. And the casket is that great, perfect box you've been looking for your whole life.

What Really Matters?

It's not bad to play the game. It's not bad to be really good at it. It's not bad to be Master of the Board. My grandmother taught me to play to win. But there are always more rungs to climb, more money to be made, more deals to pull off. And the danger is that we forget to ask what really matters. We race around the board with shallow relationships, frenzied schedules, preoccupied souls. Being smart or strong does not protect you from this fate. In some ways, it makes the game more dangerous, for the temporary rewards you get from playing can lull you into pretending that the game will never end.

As a student in school, I may think that the game is won by getting better grades or making first string or getting elected class president. Then comes graduation and the pressure to win at my job, to get promoted, to have enough money to feel safe, and to be able to think of myself as successful. I pass somebody up and feel pleasure. Someone passes me, and I feel a stab of pain. Always I hear this inner voice: *Is it enough? Did I do good?* And sometimes if I'm quiet: *Does it mean anything?*

Then the chase is for financial security, a well-planned retirement in an active senior community where Botox and Grecian Formula and ginko biloba and Lipitor and Viagra bring chemically induced temporary immortality.

> Then one day it stops.
> For you, the game is over.
> Did you play wisely?

Then one day it stops. Other people keep going. Somewhere on the board, somebody is just getting started. But for you, the game is over. Did you play wisely? We all want God, Anne Lamott writes, but left to our own devices, we seek all the worldly things — possessions, money, looks, and power — because we think they will bring us fulfillment. "But this turns out to be a joke, because they are just props, and when we check out of this life, we have to give them all back to the great prop master in the sky. They're just on loan. They're not ours." They all go back in the box.

Live Differently — Starting Now

Human beings are the only creatures whose frontal lobes are so developed that they know that the game will end. This is our glory, our curse, our warning, and our opportunity. In Jerusalem, hundreds of synagogues have been built by Jews from around the world. One was built by a group from Budapest, and according to an ancient custom, they had a coffin built into the wall. There is no body in it, they explain to visitors; it is present as a silent witness to remind us that it all goes back in the box.

The Talmud teaches that every person should fully repent one day before his death. When a visitor asked, "But how will I know when that day is?" he was told: "Treat every day as if it were the day before your last." Arrange your life around what matters most. Starting today. The box will wait.

This is how my grandmother taught me to play the game of my life, and I talk about that in the pages that follow. My grandmother led, in many ways, a pretty simple life. She never went to high school, never led a company, never wrote a book, never traveled the world. She met her lifelong sweetheart in the eighth grade, her last year of formal education. She gave birth to three sons named—I'm not making this up—Hack, Jack, and Mac (the names Huey, Dewey, and Louie already having been taken by Donald Duck's nephews), and then three girls, including my mother. She never moved outside the state where she was born. The only paid job she ever had that I know of was working behind the counter in a little Swedish bakery.

She was content with her life because she believed she knew what mattered. She had a clear understanding about what she thought was temporal and what was eternal. Everybody has to decide what he or she believes constitutes winning and losing in life. One of the smartest men who ever lived told one of his most unforgettable stories about exactly that decision. That's for the next chapter. But I have had a long time to think about it.

My grandmother taught me how to play the game.

THE OBJECT

CHAPTER 2

BE RICH
TOWARD GOD

I intend to live forever. So far, so good.

STEVEN WRIGHT

We make a living by what we get.
We make a life by what we give.

DAVE TOYCEN

Once upon a time in Silicon Valley there lived a busy, important man. He routinely logged twelve- to fourteen-hour days at his job, and sometimes weekends. He picked up an MBA and joined professional organizations and boards of directors to expand his contacts. He listened to business books on keeping up with the sharks and leadership lessons from Ghengis Khan on a special CD player in his car that sped up the reader's voice so he could get through it in half the normal time. Even when he was not working, his mind drifted toward his work so that it was not only his occupation but also his preoccupation. He found the forty-hour work week such a good idea he would often do it twice a week.

His wife tried to slow him down, to remind him that he had a family. He knew that they were not as close as they once had been. He had not intended to drift away. It's just that she always seemed to want *time* from him, and that is what he did not have to give. He gave at the office.

He was vaguely aware that his kids were growing up and he was missing it. From time to time his children would complain about books that he wasn't reading to them, games of catch he wasn't playing with them, lunches he wasn't eating with them. But after a while they stopped complaining, because they stopped expecting that their lives might ever be different.

I'll be more available to them in six months or so, he said to himself, *when things settle down.* And though he was a very bright guy, he didn't seem to notice that things never settled down. *Besides,* he said to himself when he felt guilty, *I'm doing it all for them.* Of course this was not even partly true. He would have lived this way if they didn't exist at all. He lived this way even though they begged him to change. But because they didn't move out to live in a cardboard box, because they lived in the home and ate the food and wore the clothes and played the video games that his money provided, he could say to himself, *I'm doing it all for them.* And no one knew him or loved him enough to tell him the truth.

He knew that he was not taking great care of his body. His doctor told him he had some pretty serious warning signs — elevated blood pressure, high cholesterol — and told him he needed to cut down on the Twinkies and red meat and start an exercise program. So he stopped going to his doctor. *There will be plenty of time for that,* he said to himself, *when things settle down.*

He recognized that his life was out of balance. His wife nagged him about going to church — there was one down the street from them. He intended to go, but Sunday morning was the only time he could crash. He prided himself on being a practical man who lived in the real world where money is how you keep score. *Besides, I can be spiritual without going to church,* he said to himself. *There will be plenty of time for that sort of thing when things settle down.*

One day the chief operations officer of his company came to see him. "You won't believe this, but things are booming to such an extent that we can't keep up. It's a miracle. This is our chance to catch the mother lode. If we catch this wave, we will be set for life. But it will require major changes. We have inventory headaches you would not believe. Orders are coming in so fast that supply can't keep pace with demand. Our software is hopelessly outdated. If we don't over-haul this operation from top to bottom, it will be a disaster."

Then it hit him. He would put his company through a technologi-cal revolution. They would go completely wireless—24/7 accessibility for everyone, universally mandatory hands-free phones, and fax ma-chines in the employees' washrooms. He thought up a new company motto—"We live for this!"—and had it printed on everything.

This was the opportunity of a lifetime. He was now available to everyone in the world except for those who needed him most, and whom he needed most—his wife, his children, himself, his friends, his God.

He said to his wife that night, "Do you realize what this means? We can relax. Our future is assured—we're set for life. I know the market; I've covered every base, anticipated every contingency. This means financial security. We can finally go on that vacation you've been pestering me about."

He was Master of the Board. But his wife had heard this sort of thing before; she had learned not to get her hopes up. At 11:00 she went up to bed by herself—as usual.

Life, Interrupted

As the Master of the Board sat before his terminal rearranging the universe, there was only one microscopic detail that escaped his at-tention. An artery that had once been as supple as a blade of grass was now as dry as plaster and as stiff as old cement. The blood cells could barely squeeze through. Every day, while the man made plans, drafted urgent memos, anxiously checked his portfolio, artfully fi-nessed his board, a few more chips of lipids and debris joined the plaque block. Every cigar, every pat of butter, every angry word, every irritation-filled drive in the car, every self-preoccupied thought had done its work. Quietly, efficiently, irresistibly, his body was preparing to do him in.

For more than half a century his heart had been pumping 70 milliliters of blood with every contraction, 14,000 pints each day, 100,000 beats every 24 hours—all without his ever sending it a memo or giving it a performance review. Now it skipped a beat. Then another. And a third. He gasped for air and clutched his chest. For a moment he was given the gift of blinding clarity. Even though he sat at the top of a hundred org charts, it turns out he wasn't even in control of his own pulse. Funny thing: thousands of employees on multiple continents would obey his every word with fear and trembling. But a few ounces of recalcitrant muscle brought him to his knees. *Now I lay me down to sleep. . . .*

> *Even though he sat at the top of a hundred org charts, it turns out he wasn't even in control of his own pulse.*

His wife woke up at 3:00 a.m., and he was still not beside her. She went downstairs to drag him to bed and saw him still sitting in front of the computer terminal, his head on his desk. *This is ridiculous,* she said to herself. *It's like being married to a child. He would rather fall asleep in front of a screen than come to bed.*

She touched him on the shoulder to wake him up, but he did not respond, and his skin was alarmingly cold. Panicking, she felt a sick feeling in her stomach as she dialed 911. When the paramedics got there, they told her that he had suffered a massive heart attack, that he had already been dead for hours.

His death was a major story in the financial community. His obituary was written up in *Forbes* and the *Wall Street Journal*. It's too bad he was dead, because he would have loved to read what they wrote about him.

Then came the memorial service. Because of his prominence, the whole community turned out. People filed past his casket and made the same foolish comment people always make at funerals: "He looks so peaceful." Rigor mortis will do that. Death is nature's way of telling you to slow down. They ask the same foolish question people ask when somebody rich dies: "I wonder how much he left." He left it all. Everybody always leaves it all.

People got up to eulogize him. Mostly, they talked about his accomplishments, because while everybody knew *about* him, no one really knew *him*.

"He was one of the leading entrepreneurs of his day," said one.

"He was an innovator of technology and delivery systems," said another.

"He was a man of principles," somebody else said; "he would never cheat on his taxes, his expense account, or his wife."

Another admirer noted his civic achievements: "He was a pillar in the community. He knew everybody. This man was a networker."

They had commissioned a large marble memorial column for him. On it they wrote all these inspiring words: *Visionary. Innovator. Leader. Entrepreneur.* And at the top they wrote this word, the man's favorite word, the word he'd given his soul for: *Success.* They put up the man's memorial stone, buried his body, and went home.

Then when it was dark and no one was present to note what was taking place, the angel of God was sent to this cemetery. Unseen and unheard, the angel made his way past all the other tombstones until he came to the man's wonderful memorial stone. There the angel traced with a finger the single word God had chosen to summarize this wealthy, busy, respectable, successful man's life: *Fool.*

God said, "You fool. This very night your soul will be required of you. And the things you have stored up—whose will they be?"

The Diagnosis

By now you may have recognized this is a version of a story first told by Jesus two thousand years ago, and Jesus was very frank in his diagnosis. He doesn't say the man was evil or wicked. He just calls him a fool.

Why does Jesus use this harsh word? This man did not deliberately set out to neglect his wife or ignore his kids. He didn't establish the goal of becoming as greedy and self-preoccupied as possible. He didn't purpose in his heart to defy God or close off all compassion for the poor. He just had other things to do. He was too busy.

He just devoted his life to the wrong things. If you were to make a list of his priorities, it would look something like this:

What Matters Most

1. Harvest large crop
2. Build bigger barns
3. Achieve financial security
4. Eat
5. Drink
6. Be merry
7. Remember not to die

And of course, the last item is the really hard one. Sooner or later our souls will return to their Maker. And the things you have stored up—whose will they be? This was the realization that tormented Solomon: "I hated all the things I had toiled for under the sun, because I must leave them to the one who comes after me." "The executive who works from 7:00 a.m. to 7:00 p.m. every day will be both very successful and fondly remembered by his wife's next husband," author John Capozzi writes, and he could be speaking about our man.

Lisa Rotgrak is the author of a book called *Death Warmed Over*, a combination cookbook and sociological study of funeral meals and rituals. She starts it with the story of a man dying at home in bed. He could smell the aroma of chocolate chip cookies—his favorite—baking downstairs. He wanted one more cookie before he died.

He dragged his body out of bed, rolled down the stairs, crawled into the kitchen, and reached out a trembling arm to grasp one final cookie, when he felt the sting of a spatula smack his hand. "Put that back," his wife said. "They're for the funeral."

> The rich fool had many cookies, and he thought they were all for him.

The rich fool had many cookies, and he thought they were all for him. "This is what I'll do," says the rich fool. "I will tear down my barns and build bigger ones, and there I will store all my grain and my goods."

One more barn. One more crop. One more cookie. Then one night out comes the spatula. *Whack.* "They don't belong to you. They're for the funeral."

Ask not for whom the spatula whacks. It whacks for thee.

The Object of the Game

When Jesus told his story, he summed up the lesson in a single sentence to make sure no one missed the point: "So it is for everyone who accumulates riches for themselves but are not rich toward God."

The object of life, according to Jesus, is breathtakingly simple: *Be rich toward God.* Don't spend your life playing Master of the Board. It's a sucker's game. You can't beat the house. But you can be *rich toward God.* Your life — with God's help — can be a source of pleasure to the God of the universe. You can make God smile.

When the game is over, all that will matter will be God's assessment of our lives. Venture capitalists and Hollywood stars and school janitors and Somalian tribesmen will stand in line before him on level ground.

> Being rich toward God means growing a soul that is increasingly healthy and good.
>
> Being rich toward God means loving and enjoying the people around you.
>
> Being rich toward God means learning about your gifts and passions and doing good work to help improve the world.
>
> Being rich toward God means becoming generous with your stuff.
>
> Being rich toward God means making that which is *temporary* become the servant of that which is *eternal.*
>
> Being rich toward God means savoring every roll of the dice and every trip around the board.

Each of these dimensions of richness matters, and we will spend whole chapters looking at them in more depth. But Jesus expressed it in two great commandments, each built around a single word: *Love.*

Love God with all your heart, soul, mind, and strength, he said. Love your neighbor as yourself. Everything else is commentary. No one can do this and be poor in God's eyes. No one can fail to do this and be rich in God's eyes.

Loving God

Being rich toward God begins with giving to God that which he desires most of all. And what he desires most from you is *you*—your heart and devotion. Just as God can give us many gifts but the best gift is himself, so we can offer God our resources and acts of service, but the gift he desires most is us.

I think of Jesus' last conversation with his friend Peter. Peter was so human: he followed Jesus, served him, learned from him, doubted him, misunderstood him, praised him, and denied him, but Jesus' final question for his friend was only this: "Peter, do you love me?" Three times he asked Peter this question. He would go on to tell Peter what he wanted Peter to *do*, but what he wanted most was love. Augustine said that all ethics can be summed up in this: "Love God, and do what you will," for the soul that truly loves God will want to do what God loves.

An illustration may help us understand this concept. My wife and I had been through a busy few weeks: heavier than usual travel commitments, out-of-town guests staying with us, and some unscheduled complications. So Nancy sat me down and said, "I want to spend the day with you. Just the two of us."

It's a strange thing. There's no one I enjoy being with more. But because I felt so busy, I made a counteroffer. "How about if we spend the morning each working on our own tasks and then are together from lunch on?"

At first she agreed. Then she returned and put her foot (also known as "the hammer") down: "No working. No meetings. We're spending the whole day together; having a great time, or there's going to be trouble."

So we spent the whole day together. We didn't do anything fancy. We did the things we usually do. We went for a drive, we took a walk, we had lunch, we talked about stuff. It was an ordinary day. And that was just what she wanted to do.

Do you think Nancy would have been any happier if I had fixed her breakfast in bed, massaged her feet for an hour, brought her flowers, and watched back-to-back episodes of *Oprah* with her?

Well, we'll never know.

But it struck me that in a sense the story of the Bible is the story of a single desire of God: the reason God created people is so he could be with us. In Eden he would come and walk with the man and woman he had made, just to be with them. Then after the fall, we experienced separation from God. And it's as if from that moment God was haunted by his desire to be with people. Many times in Scripture we read that God would "be with" individuals: he walked with Enoch and Noah; he was with Abraham and Isaac; he was with Joseph in slavery and in prison. He formed a nation so he could have a people to be with: "Then I will dwell among the Israelites and be their God. They will know that I am the LORD their God, who brought them out of Egypt so that I might dwell among them."

> *It's as if from that moment God was haunted by his desire to be with people.*

God still was not satisfied. He got an idea: "I'm going down." One day a baby was born in Bethlehem. He grew up and called any human beings who would to follow him. "He appointed twelve — designating them apostles — that they might be with him." And he made this offer: "Anyone who loves me will obey my teaching. My Father will love them, and we will come to them and make our home with them."

The lonely soul is poor. The "with-God" soul is rich. The reason God made you is because he wants to be with you. And we don't have to wait. It's as if each day God is saying, "I'd like to spend day with you."

It's a funny thing. I believe in God. I believe there is no one else worth giving my life to. But sometimes, because I feel busy, or hurried, or selfish, or just sinful — I want to make a counteroffer.

I cannot *make* myself love God more by sheer willpower. But I can choose to be with him. I ask him to go through the day with me when I wake up. I learn to see his goodness in creation and beauty. I take time to ask for his help as we work together. I see him in the people with whom I meet. I hear his voice in what I read. I ask his forgiveness for the many times I mess up. I thank him at the end of the day for his presence in it.

I can't make myself love God, but I can come to know him better. And because God is love, the more I come to know him, the more my love for him will grow. Love is a by-product of knowing. So I can spend this day loving God. And tomorrow I can seek to love him a little more. This is a life "rich toward God."

Loving People

When I was in Ethiopia recently, I was struck, as so many Westerners are, by the grinding poverty. While I was there, though, a man told me, "In the West, you measure a man's wealth by his possessions. In this country, we measure his wealth by his friends." How will you measure your wealth?

Pastor Bill Hybels wrote recently about a meeting at which a speaker stood in front of a large group of people with a roll of stickers in his hand. Behind him on the platform were tables filled with props that represented the stuff of our lives — a Matchbox car, a dollhouse, a tiny desk that stood for our jobs.

                    med the stage and placed a red sticker on each

                the crowd that they may not be able to see it

              e sitting, but each sticker contained the same

             e said, "Everything that I'm putting a sticker on

            not last. It will fade away. We invest our emotions

            en we acquire it, it gives us a little thrill. And we

think the thrill will last. But it does not. It fades. And eventually, so will what we acquire.

"If you are living for what you see up here, then you are living for what is temporary. Temporary satisfaction, temporary fulfillment, temporary meaning. It will come to an end—but you never will. It will leave you with a terrible emptiness."

Bill watched as the speaker plastered red stickers on everything sitting on the stage. He walked before the now silent room, pronouncing with his hands the ultimate fate of the greatest goods this world has to offer. It's the word that never appears in ads on TV or the temptations that play out in our soul. It's the word that might have saved the rich fool in Jesus' story, if only he had plastered it on his barns and crops. *Temporary. Temporary. Temporary. Temporary. Temporary. Temporary. Temporary. Temporary.*

"There is only *one* thing in this room that is not temporary," he went on. "There is only one item that you will be allowed to take with you from this life into the next."

He had a little girl join him on stage, and he put a blue sticker on the collar of her dress. "When you get to the end of your life and take in your last breath, what do you want your life to have been about? What will make it rich in the eyes of God?"

People.

Wise people build their lives around what is eternal and squeeze in what is temporary. Not the other way around. So let's try an exercise in understanding what is at stake. Think for a few moments about two categories: "forever" and "temporary." What in your life is going to last forever, and what is going back in the box?

Now take it a step further. In your imagination (or it might be helpful for you to do this in real life), take a pad of self-adhesive notes and write "TEMPORARY" on each one. Walk around and distribute them everywhere you need to be reminded. Put one on your car. Put one on the front door of your house. Put TEMPORARY stickers on each piece of furniture. Put one on the front of your checkbook. Stick them on all the clothes in your closet. Put them on your iPod and on

Forever	Going back in the box
God	Possessions
Other people	My resume
My soul	My body
Deeds of love	Money
	Pleasures
	Other people's opinions of me
	Security
	Titles and positions
	Youth
	Power
	Physical attractiveness
	Health

the TV and the treadmill and the barbeque.

Then take another set of self-adhesive notes and write "ETERNAL." Put them on your family. Put them on your friends. Put one on your boss. Put one on the stranger behind the counter. Put one on the person you most dislike in the world. Don't forget to put one on your forehead as well.

For the stuff in our lives is only temporary. The day is coming when all our 401(k)s and our bank statements will be irrelevant. The titles on our resumes will no longer impress anyone. GPAs and SAT scores and college acceptances will be long-forgotten. No one will know what clothes hung in our closets or what cars sat in our garages.

All that will be left is love. That which was done out of love for God will last. Every human being you see is a cleverly disguised receptacle of eternity. You can take the love with you.

The object of life is to be rich toward God.

SETUP

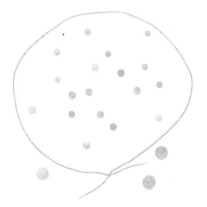

CHAPTER 3

THREE WAYS
TO KEEP SCORE

> Some wonderful, dazzling successes are going to happen
> for some of the most awful, angry, undeserving people you know —
> people who are, in other words, not you.
>
> **ANNE LAMOTT**

Robert Roberts writes about a fourth grade class in which the teacher introduced a game called the "balloon stomp." A balloon was tied to every child's leg. When the signal was given, the object of the game was for the students to try to pop everybody else's balloon while protecting their own. The last child with an intact balloon would be the winner.

Balloon stomp is a zero-sum game. If I win, you lose. Anyone else's successes diminish my chances. I must regard everyone else as someone to overcome, someone to be pitted against.

Balloon stomp is a Darwinian contest, the survival of the fittest. Some ten-year-olds are pretty Darwinian, and they entered into the spirit of the thing vigorously. Balloons were relentlessly targeted and destroyed. Some children pretended to be enjoying the game but were secretly afraid of losing. A few of the children hung shyly on the sidelines, but that didn't help them. Their balloons were doomed just the same. The battle was over in a matter of seconds. Only one balloon was still inflated, and of course its owner was the most (secretly) disliked kid in the room. It's hard to really win at balloon stomp.

Then, Roberts writes, a disturbing thing happened. A second class was brought in the room to play the same game, only this time it was a class of developmentally challenged children. They too were each given a balloon and the same instructions. The same signal began the game. "I got a sinking feeling in my midsection," said one of the onlookers. "I wanted to spare the kids the pressure of a competitive brawl."

Only this time the game proceeded differently. The instructions were given too quickly to be grasped very well by these children; out of the confusion the one idea that sunk in was that the balloons were supposed to be popped. But instead of fighting each other off, these children got the idea that they were supposed to help one another pop balloons. So they formed a kind of "balloon stomp co-op." One boy was getting frustrated because the balloon he was going after wouldn't hold still enough for him to pop it. So the little girl to whom it was tied knelt down and held her balloon carefully in place, like the holder for a field-goal kicker, while the little boy stomped it flat. Big smile. Then he knelt down and held his balloon still for her to stomp. On and on it went, all the children helping one another in the Great Stomp.

And when the very last balloon was popped, everybody cheered. Everybody won.

What happened was that they had actually devised a brilliant alternative scoring system. In the new system, students didn't score points *against* each other but *with* each other. People who looked at each other as opponents in the old system became teammates in the new one. People who looked like losers in the old system became winners in the new one.

So who got the game right, and who got the game wrong? What's the best way to keep score?

We All Are Scorekeepers

The first question you ask when you arrive at a game already in progress is "What's the score?" The score defines reality. When our children were very young, one of them played on a soccer team that had a tough year. Not only did our team not win a single game all season, but we did not score a single goal. All season. Stomp.

All games involve score keeping. The rules of scoring in any game tell the players which achievements count; what to do in order to be a winner. Monopoly players keep score with money; football players count touchdowns; poker players use chips. In most games, players want to score as high as possible; in golf the object is to have the lowest score. The British keep score in cricket, but no one has figured out how. Or why.

> *We are, by nature, scorekeepers.... Our behavior is inevitably aimed at achieving a higher point total.*

We are, by nature, scorekeepers. We crave feedback. We want to know how we're doing. Is my life on track? Am I doing what matters? Our sense of the score exerts a powerful influence over our lives. Our behavior is inevitably aimed at achieving a higher point total.

To talk about how we keep score is really to talk about how we define success. But we do not start out in life inventing the scoring system on our own. We learn about it from others.

One of the important questions about our story is this: "As I have gone through my life from childhood to the present, who have been my most important scorekeepers?" For most of us, the first important scorekeepers in our lives are our parents. We want to know how to win their smiles, attention, and approval. Perhaps our teachers are next. Report cards are one of the ways children keep score. Coaches teach us to keep score, as do our peers. Later on it's our bosses, or coworkers, or neighbors.

Score Keeping in the Bible

The Bible is full of characters who found ways to keep score of their lives. Score keeping goes back at least to Cain and Abel. We are told that Abel's burnt offering found favor with God but that Cain's offering—presumably because it did not line up with God's commands—did not. So "Cain was very angry, and his face was downcast." He kept score by comparing his spiritual status with that of his brother. And losing made him mad enough to kill.

Rachel and Leah were both married to Jacob. Rachel was lovely in face and form, but Leah had weak eyes. Rachel was the one Jacob loved, but Leah was the one having babies. After Leah had given birth to three children, Rachel was mad enough to spit. So she told Jacob to sleep with her servant girl so that she could at least have a child on her side of the ledger, and Jacob went along. After this arrangement had produced a few more children, Leah told Jacob to sleep with her servant so that she would get back in the win column. Once again, Jacob didn't put up much of a struggle. Rachel and Leah kept score by flaunting their physical attractiveness, attracting love, and having children. (They ended up tied with six sons apiece, but Leah won the tiebreaker by having a daughter as well.)

Jacob had twelve sons, but he loved his son Joseph most of all. "When his brothers saw that their father loved him more than any of them, they hated him and could not speak a kind word to him." They kept score by seeing who was the family favorite.

Saul was a mighty king, but when he came home from battle, the women danced in the streets to a new song: "Saul has slain his thousands, and David his tens of thousands." And from that day on, Saul kept an evil eye on David. Saul kept score by number of kills and popularity with the most people.

The rich fool in Jesus' story said to himself, "You have plenty of good things laid up for many years. Take life easy; eat, drink and be merry." He was keeping score with his money.

Our behavior will be dictated by whatever scoring system we are hooked up to emotionally. We need that inner sense of worth and well-being. The question is, how satisfied are we with the system we're living with? Most commonly we tend to keep score with the three Cs: comparing, competing, and climbing.

Comparing To

One of the ways we keep score is by comparison. Psychologists say people engage in three types of comparing. They compare their situation to those who are better off—*upward comparison*. They compare themselves to those at the same level—*lateral comparison*. And they compare themselves to those who are worse off—*downward comparison*. Each type carries dangers: the first incites envy, the second competition, and the third arrogance.

Not only do we tend to keep score by comparing ourselves to others, but we tend to do it in the most self-serving ways. When it comes to affluence, for instance, we tend to follow what psychologist Leon Festinger calls the "principle of slight upward comparison." We chronically compare ourselves with those just a little better off, in the hopes of attaining their level of success. This keeps us from gratitude. It also keeps our eyes off people who are underresourced so that we don't think about our need to share.

On the other hand, when it comes to ethical behavior, we all tend to compare ourselves to people we perceive to be lower than us in the morality ratings. We tend to make our ethical benchmark someone who is a little less moral than ourselves to give ourselves a higher score on integrity.

One of the main reasons we are tempted to get more invested in our work than in our relationships is that in our vocations it's easier to keep score. I can check *Forbes* magazine every year to learn who are the wealthiest four hundred people in the country. I can buy baseball cards to view an entire career on the back of a little square of cardboard. But nobody sells major league father cards with key statistics on the back ("Had a great season in 2005: set career highs in unforced expressions of affection and averaged 87 minutes of quality time per day.") How I'm doing in my relationships with other people is so much more subjective; feedback is so much fuzzier; discovering the outcome takes so much longer.

> *One of the main reasons we are tempted to get more invested in our work than in our relationships is that in our vocations it's easier to keep score.*

One national magazine just printed a list of the world's one hundred most powerful women; a financial journal listed the world's four hundred wealthiest people; *Time* recently devoted a cover story to the twenty-five most influential Hispanics in the United States; *People* annually features lists of the most beautiful people; the television channel VH1 is running a show on *Maxim's* one hundred hottest women — all evidence that the old categories of money, sex, and power are still pretty high in the world scoring system.

Students compare test scores, GPAs, SAT scores, and college acceptances. In our vocations, we compare salaries, titles, org chart status, promotions, and office size and location. Did I get compliments on my physical appearance? Does someone think I'm smart, or funny?

These things can happen inside churches as well as outside. I happen to understand this particular score-keeping method quite well. Years ago I was at a pastors' conference. During a break between sessions, three of us were talking together. One man said to another, "So, how is your church going?" In case you're not a pastor, let me translate. That's pastorese for "How big is your church?" which is pastorese for "How important are you? Are you worthwhile for me to talk to and get to know? Would it be cool to go back home and tell people I had a conversation with you?"

The pastor responded: "Oh, pretty good. We have about 1,000 at our church. How's your church going?"

The first pastor said, "Well, the Lord's blessing us all right. We run around 1,500 or so."

Then they looked at me. I knew what was coming next.

I was working at a church that had maybe 250 attendees at the time. And then a little voice, so quiet I was hardly even aware of it, began to whisper some management impression strategy to me: *Say the church has about 300 people. 250 people is awfully small. A church of 300 people sounds less embarrassing than only 250.*

Right at the same time, another inner voice responded: *What are you doing? You don't even know these men. You will never see them again. Do you think they'd really care? Are you willing to trade your integrity, which when you come right down to it, is all you really have, for the sake of the status you would gain by 50 lousy people?*

So I said we run about 2,000. Not just transfers from other churches, either. Seriously impressive converts — Hugh Hefner, Jimmy Hoffa, the Dalai Lama.

The tug to score the wrong kind of points pulls at me more often than I can say.

Competing With

Another scoring system is competition, in which one person is not just perceiving himself or herself relative to another — comparison — but actually trying to best the other. I don't think competition itself is a bad thing. In fields from athletics to business, competitors can challenge one another to heights of performance and excellence they did not know they had the ability to attain. As we will see later, competition can spur us to new levels of determination and persistence and a spirit that never says die.

But competition becomes toxic when it gives rise to envy and jealousy. It becomes dark when I am tempted to cheat in order to come out ahead. It poisons the soul when "winner" and "loser" become labels of worth and identity, and respect for the battle itself is lost.

In sports and business and almost everything else, the question we ask is, "Who's number one?" We become obsessed with this: "Am I the best? The fastest? The smartest?" No sports arena sells a giant foam core hand holding up two fingers.

We can turn everything into competition. Amazon.com offers a service whereby authors can find out where their books rank in total sales against every other book in the world. It gets updated every day. I can score myself against other authors by a number that tells me whether I'm winning or losing. In the words of novelist Gore Vidal, "It is not enough to succeed. Others must fail." Score keeping has never before been this immediate. Jeremiah never checked out *Israel Today* to see if he had passed up Isaiah on the nonfiction bestseller list. William Shakespeare didn't look to see how many copies of his plays Christopher Marlowe sold.

I look up the rank of an author in an occupation similar to mine, who writes on similar topics, and find that his book has a better ranking than mine. My immediate response is to feel depressed. There is nothing good in this response.

Not every society is so competitive. One anthropologist described organizing games for Australian Aboriginal children. They so disliked "disgracing" each other that the faster runners would deliberately slow down to encourage the slower ones. Writer-ecologist Jay Griffiths notes that in Brazil the Xavante people have a ritual involving two sets of people carrying heavy logs. To Western observers it looks like a race, but if one group falls behind, the other will wait for them so they can complete the run together. Trying to figure out who won is like asking who wins a ballet. It's about helping, not beating.

> To Western observers the rite looks like a race.... We can even turn spirituality into a competition.

We can even turn spirituality into a competition. Harold Kushner wrote about a very bright, driven pre-med student at a very competitive college. While traveling in the East the summer before his junior year, he met a guru who said, "Don't you see you're poisoning your soul with this success-oriented way of life? Your idea of happiness is to stay up all night studying for an exam so you can get a better grade than your best friend. Your idea of a good marriage is not to find the woman who will match your soul, but to win the girl everybody else wants. That is not how people are supposed to live. Come join us in an atmosphere where we all share and love one another."

He was ripe for this. He called his parents and told them he was dropping out of school to live in an ashram. Six months later, they received a letter from him:

> Dear Mom and Dad,
>   I know you weren't happy about my decision, but I want to tell you how it has changed me. For the first time in my life, I'm at peace. Here there is no competing, no trying to get ahead of anyone.

This way of life is so in harmony with my inner soul that in only six months I've become the #2 disciple in the entire community, and I think I can be #1 by June.

Climbing Above

Some years ago I had lunch with a businessman who was, by almost any scoring system, a very successful man. He was probably about fifty, had been involved in real estate development, and had an amazing knack for seizing opportunities.

He was playing a game that might be called "Climbing up the Ladder." Every rung up the ladder was another point. He knew how to climb the ladder, and he climbed it really well. I was fresh out of grad school, making very little money and still in debt for my education. He pulled up in a brand-new silver jaguar convertible.

I said, "Wow." I had no idea people actually drove something like that.

I was driving a ten-year-old pretty badly beat-up Honda Accord. Worse, it had been in an accident. To keep the passenger door firmly closed, I had to rig the seat belt through the handle and hold on to it with my right hand while steering with my left.

He said, "Wow." He had no idea people actually drove something like that.

He told me how when he was starting out in business, he would often read profiles in *Forbes* or the *Wall Street Journal* of successful entrepreneurs and CEOs who were higher up on the ladder than him, and those stories would fuel his drive.

They would motivate him to work a little harder, climb a little faster. Then something happened. These profiles almost always include the person's age. One day he noticed that he was reading about somebody who was very successful, who had climbed the ladder higher than he had, only this man was younger than he was. He felt a little pang. He realized that as long as the stories were about somebody older, he could tell himself that the only reason he was lower than they were is that he was younger. It was just a matter of time before he passed them up.

Now there was somebody on a faster track than him. As the years went by, there were more stories about guys who were younger who had climbed higher. He got a little depressed every time he read one.

Know what he did? He stopped reading the stories. They made him feel bad. The ladder wasn't good to him. His marriage was on life support. His kids' lives were a mess. He went to church and sat in the same pew every week, but he held himself back. No one knew him. He never opened up his heart. Because the truth was: the ladder was his game. The ladder was his family. The ladder was his god.

When he was younger, every time he reached a new rung, he would feel a little twinge of pleasure. But it never lasted. He always had to climb more. He found — as people generally find — that when he got older, the going got slower. The rungs got farther apart. The ladder became more crowded. Though he was a smart guy, he couldn't bring himself to get off the ladder. He was afraid.

We live in Ladderville. Once you get on one, it's very hard to get off. We look at people higher up on the ladder and feel discontent. We don't look at people lower on the ladder much. When you are climbing a ladder, you face upwards.

Recently I was listening to a radio preacher talking about the need for gratitude. He was at an inner-city church, and he exhorted his congregation to "be thankful you had enough money to get here on the bus." When you're climbing the ladder, you tend to think about people who have nicer cars than yours. You don't think about people who have to ride the bus — that might make me have second thoughts about my drive to keep climbing.

How Does God Keep Score?

We had a service at our church once where the grounds were covered with ladders, inside the church and outside. We will never do it again, because I must have had a dozen people ask me if the sermon was going to be about ladder-day saints.

We were actually talking about a passage of Scripture where Paul talks about how God keeps score. He says: "Your attitude should be the same as that of Christ Jesus: Who, being in very nature God, did not consider equality with God something to be grasped, but made himself nothing, taking the very nature of a servant."

The entire life of Jesus isn't the story of somebody climbing *up* a ladder; it's a picture of someone coming down—a series of demotions. To begin with, Jesus was "in very nature God." He was at the top of the organizational chart of the universe. But he did not consider this to be "grounds for grasping"; he gave up the right to have things his own way and became a servant. But even angels are servants, so he went lower: he became a human being. He took on flesh and blood, all our needs and limitations. This is the beauty of the incarnation— God coming down. But even on a human level, some people live as kings and celebrities, so Jesus took another demotion: he "humbled himself" and was born in a stable as the peasant son of a penniless couple. But even that was not low enough. He kept going down by becoming "obedient to death." His ultimate task wasn't some glorious achievement. There was nothing glamorous about death. But his demotion didn't stop there. He went one rung lower: "even death on a cross."

> This is the beauty of the incarnation— God coming down.

The problem with spending your life climbing up the ladder is that you will go right past Jesus, for he's coming down.

And ironically, the moment he looked most like a failure in the world scoring system was his moment of greatest triumph in the eyes of the Father. "Therefore God exalted him to the *highest* place and gave him the name that is above every name."

Serving in self-giving love is the most Godlike thing a human being can do. So Jesus played another game. It was called "foot washer." People wore sandals or went barefoot in his day. Roads were filled with dust and dirt and worse. Foot washing was a slave's job.

Occasionally a child might do it for a parent as an act of devotion. There is one ancient story of a wife doing it for her husband. There is no story of a superior doing it for his servants or of a rabbi for his students.

Jesus gathered the disciples to eat. Maybe they were wondering who was supposed to get the foot washer. Jesus picked up a towel and a basin of water and began to wash his disciples' feet. When he knelt before Peter, Peter tried to stop him. But Jesus said it was necessary. When he finished, the disciples were speechless, their heads hanging.

In the new game, people who try to make themselves servants— humbly, honestly, and joyfully—keep getting revealed as the biggest winners. People who recognize and embrace their smallness keep getting bigger and bigger in God's eyes. It's the oddest scoring system.

CHAPTER 4

MASTER
THE INNER GAME

If you live to be one hundred, you've got it made.
Very few people die past that age.

GEORGE BURNS
(WHO LIVED TO BE ONE HUNDRED, THEN DIED)

I grew up playing tennis with my dad and then taught tennis during college and grad school. Because we were both readers, our house was filled with books about tennis. But the best one, the racquet bible, was called *The Inner Game of Tennis*. The author was a former Harvard tennis captain who said, "Every game is composed of two parts, an outer game and an inner game. The outer game is played against an external opponent to overcome external obstacles, and to reach an external goal." To master the outer game, we must learn to swing a racquet or a club or a bat. The outer game is what people see, what gets admired or disdained or ignored.

But there is another, more important game going on in the mind of the player. It is played against nervousness, doubt, and self-condemnation. It requires the offering of the will and the focus of the mind. Victories at the inner game are the source of all true joy and growth. The possibility of inner mastery is the highest reason why we play the game.

I think of this distinction when I read the words of Paul to the church at Corinth. He was rotting away in prison. His enemies were gloating. The outer game didn't seem to be going well. But he wrote that he was a jar of clay that carried great treasure: "We do not lose heart. Though outwardly we are wasting away, yet inwardly we are being renewed day by day."

Paul says that there is an outer you—your skin, hair, face, body, reputation, and persona. But there is also an inner you: Your character. Your spirit. Your soul.

The outer you is what everybody sees. It gets dressed up, applauded, whistled at, and ignored. The inner you is invisible. The outer you can be coerced by other people or forces. The inner you is always free to choose.

The outer you can be measured and weighed and chemically analyzed. The inner you has a unity and mystery that is staggering.

The outer you is temporary. The inner you is eternal.

There is something else you should know about the outer you. Paul said it like this: "Outwardly we are wasting away." Sooner or later, Old Man Wrinkle is coming for everybody.

If you have any doubts about whether or not this is true, just take a look at your best friend. Or when you're all alone, look in the mirror. From about the age of twenty-five, certain changes to the outer you start to kick in. Bones begin to lose calcium and get brittle. Skin begins to lose elasticity and shrivel. Age spots begin to multiply. You look down at your hands one day and realize you're looking at your parents' hands.

You start losing brain cells at an alarming rate. If you're over thirty, you lose thousands of brain cells every day. If you're very, very quiet, you can hear some of them dying right now.

Weight starts shifting from the poles of your body toward the equator. Hair will stop growing where you want it to and boldly go to places no hair has gone before. (I knew I was irremediably in the wasting away process a few years ago when I received not one but two nose hair trimmers from two different relatives for Christmas.)

It may be that you are not yet twenty-five. At some deep, preconscious level, you're thinking, *This will never happen to me; I will never grow old like that.*

Everyone in your life who is over thirty wants you to know they understand. They love you. But it will happen to you. And frankly, they're looking forward to it.

You can fight Old Man Wrinkle all you want. You can lavish time and money on the outer you: exercise it, starve it, Botox it, Rogaine it, stretch it, lift it, nip it, tuck it, tan it, dress it up at Neiman Marcus. One day it will just be very expensive worm food. Old Man Wrinkle will wait you out.

Who You Really Are

We can be tempted to place all our focus on the outer person. But one day all that will pass away. You, however, are a being who will never cease to exist. Your spirit—your inward character—is in process of becoming something. Something either unbelievably good or something unimaginably dark. That something is the main thing God sees when he looks at us. That's what matters most to him.

One time God sent his prophet Samuel to anoint someone who would become king. The prophet saw a very impressive looking outer person and thought, *This must be the guy*. But God said: "Do not consider his appearance or his height, for I have rejected him. The LORD does not look at the things man looks at. Man looks at the outward appearance, but the LORD looks at the heart."

In the New Testament, Paul says his body is headed south in a hurry. Paul had never been a movie star anyway. One of the criticisms he lived with was people saying he was not very impressive in person. And his outer person wasn't just aging; his body had been whipped and stoned and starved and beaten and locked up in a cell.

"It doesn't bother me much," he said, "'cause my body's just kind of a loaner anyhow. Rent-a-wreck material. It's what's inside that matters. Something's going on inside of me; it's like the opposite of what's happening outside. Outside I'm dying a little every day. Inside I'm coming to life. Inside I'm growing. Changing. I keep getting stronger. Joy keeps bubbling up—even in prison. I keep getting more hopeful—even though I know my body's going to die soon. I keep loving people more—even people who put me here. It's the strangest thing: I'm dying on the outside, but inside I'm coming to life. It's fabulous." Paul had mastered the inner game. His thoughts and desires ran constantly Godward. And he found himself as an old man in prison more alive than he ever had been.

> Paul had mastered the inner game. He found himself as an old man in prison more alive than he ever had been.

There is a strange gift in aging. God, in his severe mercy, sends us daily reminders that the game will end. One author suggests that before water clocks and hourglasses, the first instrument to measure time was probably rheumatoid arthritis, that irritating sign of our fatal internal changes. The second, perhaps, was the mirror, the silent witness to the deterioration of our bodies, which is always as surprising as it is inevitable. He writes, "The hardest thing to bear as we get older is the feeling that we remain young inside." But that's only if we don't understand that outwardly we're wasting away. We will live and die in time, but we are destined for eternity.

The Picture of Dorian Gray

There is an inner game and an outer game. Which are you seeking to master? Which are you betting on? Which gets your best attention?

Oscar Wilde wrote a book called *The Picture of Dorian Gray*, the story of a man who sells his soul for ceaseless youth and beauty. Old Man Wrinkle cannot touch him. Everyone marvels at his eternal youthfulness. But his beauty hides a soul marked by greed, lust, and betrayal. A painting of him shows the condition of his inner life. Initially the face in the painting is as handsome as he is in real life. But his sin begins to be reflected on the canvas. Every act of deceit, betrayal, and greed becomes another wrinkle or pockmark or twisted feature until at last the face in the painting is too hideous to bear. He hides it in the attic. And in the end, when death comes for him, the painting is who he has become.

Dorian Gray is, in a way, the opposite of the apostle Paul. Outwardly Dorian Gray is renewed each day. Everyone envies his beauty. But inwardly he is wasting away. I wonder, when I read the book, how we might live differently if the condition of our souls were as visible as the condition of our bodies.

You don't have the painting. But you do have the soul. So if you want to know how well your soul is thriving, you will have to devote yourself to the act of reflection every once in a while. No one will pressure you to do this.

You will get inundated with messages that try to get you to obsess over the outer you. Experts tell us that if you exercise regularly, you will add two years to your life. But the bad news is that you will spend those two years exercising. Winston Churchill lived into his nineties and said the only exercise he ever got was serving as a pallbearer for his friends who died while they were exercising.

Be grateful for the outer you. Come to peace with your body. Rejoice in its strengths. Accept it in its limitations. Be grateful for it. Wash it every once in a while. Let it work hard. Be happy when it gets promoted. But remember, it's wasting away.

The inner you, on the other hand, is capable of a glory that right now you cannot even imagine. "Dear friends, now we are children of God, and what we will be has not yet been made known. But we know that when he appears, we shall be like him, for we shall see him as he is." "What we will be" — that's the inner game.

Make your biggest investment in the you that will last. We have scales and mirrors and cameras and tape measures to track the development of our outer selves. But how can we track the well-being of the part of us that will last? This may look a little different for everyone, but there are a few mirrors and scales that we all will probably need:

- Self-examination and confession
- Friends who love you enough to speak truth to you

- Time to be alone and listen to God
- Examination of your calendar and checkbook
- Key questions, such as: How easily discouraged do I get these days? How easily irritated am I compared to six months ago?
- Attention to your secret thought life. What is your mind drawn toward — really? Where do envy or blaming or judging or lusting rob your inner person of life and joy?

Mickey Mantle always expected to die very young. When he turned sixty, he commented, "If I had known I was going to live this long, I'd have taken better care of myself." You — your inner being — will live for eternity. Now is the time to start taking better care of the inner you. We have already read that Paul claimed he was being renewed every day. How? He prayed. He sang. He gave. He fellowshiped. He worshiped. He hoped. And God renewed him. Right there in prison, his inner being was strengthened in faith, hope, love, poise, wisdom, patience, gratitude, and joy. It can happen wherever the outer you happens to be. Live in such a way that you prepare yourself for eternity.

Here's a concrete place to start: spend as much time caring for the inner you as you spend on the outer you. However much time you spend exercising and cleansing and dressing the outer you this week, spend at least that much time exercising and cleansing and dressing the inner you. Notice the practices that God most uses to renew your inner person. Pay attention to the rhythms through which you become more loving and alive and resilient.

Paul asked his fellow believers in Rome, "Who shall separate us from the love of Christ? Shall trouble or hardship or persecution or famine or nakedness or danger or sword?" Well, trouble and the hard stuff can win the outer game pretty easily. But there is a you in you that no one can touch. That's the one to pay attention to.

Which game will you play?

CHAPTER 5

UNTIE
YOUR ROPES

All men want,
not something to do *with*,
but something to *be*.

HENRY DAVID THOREAU

A friend of mine, whom I will call Orville, has recently fallen in love with flying and invited me to ride along with him. He co-owns a small plane, has his pilot's license, and is trying to log as many hours as he can.

Orville is a brilliant man in many fields. He writes for a worldwide audience; he speaks for leaders of industry and finance on a regular basis; he has forgotten more than I will ever know. Flying is just one of his embarrassingly large number of competencies. But the brightest men in the world slip up every once in a while.

I met him at the small municipal airport and walked out to his plane, which was tethered to the ground by a pair of ropes that ran from the wings to metal bars embedded in the asphalt. He was going through an extremely extensive checklist, literally marking off items in a thick record book to make sure that all the safety details were taken care of: that the gas tank was full, that the wings were still firmly attached, that the signal lights worked, and so on. He was on the radio with the boys in the tower to ascertain wind and weather conditions and to get the green light to take off.

There was one part of the preflight drill I did not understand: we were still tied to the ground. The engines were roaring and the propellers were spinning, but the ropes still attached the plane wings to the earth. It seemed to me that we should loose ourselves before we took off.

I was not about to insult my friend's intelligence by mentioning this. For one thing, I know no one in the world who has less mechanical intelligence than me. If my car breaks down, I sometimes look under the hood. I have no idea why I'm doing this. If under the hood there were a giant "On-Off" switch turned to the "Off" position, I would have some idea what to do; apart from that I'm lost. So clearly there was some rope-disabling mechanism that I was not aware of. Perhaps they were tied with sophisticated slipknots that would automatically come undone when we started to taxi. Perhaps the metal bars in the ground would retract and the ropes wrap themselves up in a compartment in the wings. I was interested to find out what happened to them.

Orville finished the checklist. The tower gave us the go-ahead. He glanced out the side window and blanched: "Oh my gosh! Look at that! We haven't untied the ropes!"

I wanted to get out of the plane.

"Guess I'd better get out there and untie those ropes," he said.

I wanted to get out of the plane.

"I can't believe we were getting ready to take off without untying the ropes! That's a good one."

I wanted to get out of the plane.

My grandmother understood about the need to untie ropes also, but she called it "discarding" — getting rid of the things that will hold you back. Monopoly was a game she played with her grandchildren, but her preference ran to card games. She loved a game called canasta that required two decks of cards, and she never forgot a single card that had been played. I had a pair of twin cousins named Larry and Gary who wanted to beat my grandmother so badly they would secretly pass cards to each other using their toes. They would drop subtle hints about which suit they wanted their partner to bid in ("Boy my *heart* skipped a beat when I saw this hand"). Didn't help.

She always won. And she said the secret to the game was knowing what to discard.

In life, as in canasta, the secret lies in knowing what to discard. If I am not yet living according to what I believe matters most, it is no accident. There are forces or habits that have a deep hold on me that I will have to get rid of. The writer of Hebrews puts it like this: "Therefore, since we are surrounded by such a great cloud of witnesses, let us throw off everything that hinders and the sin that so easily entangles, and let us run with perseverance the race marked out for us."

We must discard whatever will hold us down. We must discard the wrong priorities that keep us from what matters most.

Misguided Beliefs

Maybe it's fear or doubt or a misguided sense of inadequacy. God called Moses to lead his people, but Moses wanted to ground himself. "Who am I, that I should go to Pharaoh?" Moses asked. "What if the people don't listen to me?" he complained. "I am slow of speech and tongue," he argued. He did not think his gifts were adequate for the challenge. Perhaps he pictured other leaders in his mind who were more articulate and charismatic. His image of himself as a stumbling, stuttering leader kept him tethered. Being rich toward God meant Moses would have to detach himself from his need for safety and security.

Being rich toward God meant Moses would have to detach himself from his need for safety and security.

Maybe it's a voice that wants to keep you down. One day a shepherd boy who would become King David wanted to take on a giant named Goliath who was threatening his people. David had courage and vision and audacity. He also had an older brother named Eliab who tried to talk him out of it. "Why have you come down here? And with whom did you leave those few sheep in the desert? I know how conceited you are and how wicked your heart is."

Why would Eliab say such things to his brother? Maybe he was jealous of David's heart. Perhaps David's courage made him ashamed of his own secret fear; if David soared, then Eliab would feel that much more earthbound. At any rate, Eliab was David's rope. David had to decide that placating his brother was not the ultimate goal in his life. David had to untie the rope.

Maybe it's a past mistake or failure. Maybe it's habit, comfort, or laziness. Freedom starts with naming the rope.

Classic writers on the spiritual life used to refer to this process as pursuing "detachment." That word confused me at first because it seemed to imply being remote or uninvolved with life. But actually it's just the opposite. Detachment does not mean that I am neutral, or passive, or an emotional zombie. It means that I am so committed to being rich toward God that I seek to be free of any encumbrances that could trap me. For instance, perhaps you are single and desire to be married. That may be a very good desire, but if it becomes too desperate, it needs to be discarded.

I think of a friend of mine who was so attached to getting married that she bought her wedding dress while she was still in high school. And she wasn't even dating anyone. Her very desperation to get married drove away healthy men, and the marriage she ended up jumping into was a disaster. Her urgent *attachment* to marriage not only caused her to neglect other aspects of her growth, but it kept her from the kind of mature marriage that she so badly wanted.

Sometimes our ropes are invisible to us. Although we resent their limitations, we are secretly glad they relieve us of the burden of freedom and risk. The character played by Morgan Freeman in the movie *The Shawshank Redemption* speaks of the fear of freedom in one who has been a prisoner too long: "At first, these walls, you hate them. They make you crazy. After a while you get used to 'em, don't notice 'em anymore. Then comes the day you realize you need them."

Sometimes we would rather complain about our ropes than untie them. Back in my graduate days in psychology I had a client who complained frequently about how her husband's drinking made her unhappy. "But you could take action," I suggested. "You could go to Al-Anon. You could pursue an intervention. You could tell him he must pursue sobriety or you will separate. You can begin to pursue your true life without waiting for him to sober up. You could stop providing excuses for his boss or for your friends, and the painful consequences might provoke some change."

> *Often the reason we give for not doing something is not the real reason. Sometimes we don't know what's behind the resistance.*

She batted away each of these suggestions with ease. After a while I felt like I was pitching batting practice to Barry Bonds. The truth is, she preferred the status and victimhood that goes with complaining about ropes. Her ropes obligated her friends to give her sympathy rather than hard truth. If someone were to come along and untie her ropes, she would tie them back up herself.

Sometimes we hide the *real* ropes under excuses. Jesus told a parable about a man inviting guests to a great banquet. One after the other, people tell him they cannot come. One says, "I just bought a field and I must go see it." Another says, "I just bought five yoke of oxen, and I must go check them out." But the excuses are bogus. They would be the equivalent in our day of someone saying, "I just bought a home that I haven't looked at yet, so I have to go inspect it," or "I just spent a fortune buying a car over the phone, now I have to go take a look at it." Their *real* resistance to going to the banquet — to honoring God with their lives — was something deeper than they wanted to let on.

Jesus, the master teacher, understands the way human nature works. Very often the reason we give for not doing something is not the real reason we refuse. Sometimes we don't even know ourselves what's really behind the resistance. So a helpful question can be this: "If the circumstance I'm talking about were changed, would I make a different decision? If I hadn't bought the field, would I really go to the banquet?"

Often, even after we have screwed up enough courage to untie the ropes, they tie themselves back to the ground secretly, overnight. I decide that I will spend more time with my children even if it means sacrifices at work. This may be quite an emotional decision. But the next day or the next week, I find myself still sitting at my desk while my child waits for me at home. Sometimes you have to untie the ropes every day.

The Need for Action

What does it take to untie a rope? Naming the rope is necessary but usually not sufficient. Generally it requires action. I have to stop what I'm doing, get out of the plane, and put my hands to work. One day a rich young ruler asked Jesus' advice about eternal life. After a brief discussion, Jesus offered him a chance to fly: "Go, sell all you have, give the money to the poor, and come follow me." The young man walked away sadly. He was tethered to earth by a golden rope, and he could not bring himself to untie it.

Another man knew that his rope was workaholism. It would keep him from soaring into the kind of marriage and fatherhood that he knew he longed for. For many of us, work promises to feed our egos in a way families do not. It becomes our rope. So he made a decision: every day he would leave work at 4:30. He knew that if he didn't have a set time to leave, he would always be cheating his children. He had to cut the rope, and the way he chose to do that was by setting a firm quitting time.

The particular action you choose does not have to be brilliant. It just has to be concrete. It has to cost you something. What the action consists of is not as important as taking action itself. It becomes a concrete reminder of your commitment to fly.

Orville and I left the ground, finally, and soared high above San Francisco Bay. We saw sequoias down in Muir Woods, cars racing over the Golden Gate Bridge, sunlight rippling on the waves of the Pacific Ocean, the crescent coastline of Monterey and Carmel, clouds playing tag as they raced to Napa Valley. I saw life and beauty and vision. I was glad I had flown.

But first, you have to untie your ropes.

CHAPTER 6

Resign as Master of the Board

Someone has altered the script.
My lines have been changed....
I thought I was writing this play.
MADELEINE L'ENGLE

If you want to make me laugh,
tell me your plans.
A BILLBOARD SIGNED "GOD"

It came to pass that the most powerful man in the world sat on a throne in Rome. He was devoted to acquiring and to extending his control. The world had never seen anything like it. His holdings stretched north to England, south to Africa, and east to Asia and covered more than three million square miles, more territory than the mainland United States. And he had hotels on all his properties.

This man literally ruled the known world. He ruled the rulers. He was "king of kings." His control was so unchallenged that the world was in the midst of the *pax romana*—peace of Rome. Of course, not everyone wanted to be ruled by Rome, but his army was so strong no one could challenge it.

He was very dangerous to his enemies. When that man was sixteen, the Roman orator Cicero said of him, "Octavian is a talented young man who should be praised, honored, and eliminated." But one by one, he eliminated all his rivals, until eventually he was named by the senate Caesar Augustus—we still talk about an *august* person—someone whose status is grand and majestic.

His government built statues of him to venerate. By the end of his life, people were worshiping him. Ever have that happen? Come in to work, go to your cubicle, have coworkers bow down: "Not worthy..."

Caesar did.

At one point he had a standing army of 500,000 soldiers — that took a lot of money. Caesar was a smart man, and we're told by an ancient historian that one day Caesar had an idea for how to pay his many soldiers: "And it came to pass in those days, that there went out a decree from Caesar Augustus, that all the world should be taxed."

Caesar at this time was around sixty years old. Perhaps no human being before or after ever held so much control over so much of the world so tightly for so long. "There went out a decree...." He just lifted a finger, said a word, and the whole world scrambled to obey.

Yes, Luke the historian says, watch what happens now. Now things start to get interesting. Author Tom Wright puts it like this: "This man, this king, this absolute monarch lifts his finger in Rome and 1500 miles away in an obscure province a poverty-stricken couple undertake a hazardous journey, at the whim of a king." Notice the result: a child is born in a little town that — oh, by the way — just happens to be the one mentioned in an ancient Hebrew prophecy about the coming of the Messiah.

The ancient prophecy said the Messiah would be born in Bethlehem. But Joseph and Mary didn't live in Bethlehem. They never would have gone there. Except — "it came to pass in those days, that there went out a decree from Caesar Augustus...."

Why did it come to pass?

Caesar would have told you that it was because of him. Caesar made a call. Caesar was in control. But Luke raises a question: What king is at work here? Whose will is actually being done? Who is the real Master of the Board?

Caesar thought his throne in Rome was secure. But the kingdom was lying in a manger in Bethlehem.

This account is really the tale of two cities. Rome is the site of one kind of kingdom, peace, and glory. Bethlehem is a kingdom of another kind. Money, soldiers, palaces, titles, Boardwalk, and Park Place are all in Rome. Bethlehem was all stables and mangers and donkeys and shepherds.

But the angels weren't singing in Rome. They were singing in Bethlehem.

Caesar thought his throne in Rome was as secure as a throne could be. But the kingdom was lying in a manger in Bethlehem.

Caesar has one palace left in the world. It's not in Rome but in Vegas, its glory is its glitter, and it's funded by control-deluded suckers who have yet to learn the one rule that odds makers got from John Calvin: in the long run, you can't beat the house. The baby in the manger is enthroned in hearts and lives and houses of worship on every continent in the world. How did that come to pass?

The Illusion of Control

One of the strongest of myths is the illusion of control. "I am in control" is not just a lie; author Ernest Becker called this the *vital* lie because we need it for our egos to survive. "We don't want to admit that we are fundamentally dishonest about reality, that we do not control our lives, that we always rely on something that transcends us." He says that man will use the power of money, or a string of sexual conquests, or relationships with important people, or a prestigious job, or his ability to learn, to make him feel that "he *controls* his life and death … he is a *somebody* — not just a trembling accident germinated on a hothouse planet that [Thomas] Carlyle for all time called a 'hall of doom.'"

But we are not in control.

Maybe the best commentary on this particular illusion is a book on political theory by a philosopher named Dr. Seuss. It's called *Yertle the Turtle.*

Yertle rules (or so he thinks) over a little pond of turtles. One day he decides his kingdom needs extending, so there went out a decree that all the turtles should be stacked up to become Yertle's throne.

The king lifts his hand, and the whole pond scrambles to obey. First dozens, then hundreds—he could see for miles.

Yertle thought his throne was as secure as a throne could be. But it came to pass that at the bottom of the turtle stack there was an obscure, powerless turtle named Mac.

> *That plain little Mac did a plain little thing.*
> *He burped!*
> *And his burp shook the throne of the king!*

Yertle Augustus had a great fall. And all the king's horses and all the king's men could not put Yertle together again.

For the first shall be last. And everyone who exalts himself shall be humbled. Even if you're Yertle Augustus. Even if you're Yertle VIP, MVP, PhD, CEO, BMOC—you're just one burp away from reality.

Often this "Master of the Board" delusion goes on until some external event that we cannot control punctures it. Max De Pree was a Fortune 500 company CEO and bestselling author who understood something about control, but when the life of his infant granddaughter was threatened, he wrote, "I'm seeing again—how often we need to learn this—that we can control only what counts for little. Eyesight, lungs, love, health, eternal life (you seem so on the edge to me) are gifts beyond my power to convey. How easy it is not to understand when we take something for granted."

Often it is when things are going well that we are most apt to swallow the delusion that we are in control. When Israel was on the verge of entering into the Promised Land, Moses warned them: "When you eat and are satisfied, when you build fine houses and settle down, and when your herds and flocks grow large and your silver and gold increase and all you have is multiplied, then your heart will become proud. . . . You may say to yourself, 'My power and the strength of my hands have produced this wealth for me.' But remember the LORD your God, for it is he who gives you the ability to produce wealth."

Surrender: Saying Yes to Reality

The reality of this world is that I was born into Someone Else's kingdom. My life came to me as a gift I did not choose; it is suspended from a slender thread that I did not weave and cannot on my own sustain. "Many are the plans in a human heart, but it is the LORD's purpose that prevails."

So I will need to resign as Master of the Board. The Bible's word for this is "surrender." I crown another to be Master—Lord—of my life. I offer my gifts, energies, resources, and heart to him.

> *Surrender to God is not passivity or abdication.... Surrender means I accept reality.*

Surrender is not passivity or abdication. It is saying yes to God and life each day. It is accepting the gifts he has given me—my body, my mind, my biorhythms, my energy. It is letting go of my envy or desire for what he has given someone else. It is letting go of outcomes that in reality I cannot accept anyway. I surrender my ambitions, my dreams, my money, my relationships, my marital status, my time, and my desires to God.

Surrender means I accept reality. There is a meditation that comes from another religious tradition that goes like this:

I am of the nature to grow old. There is no way to escape growing old.

I am of the nature to have ill health. There is no way to escape ill health.

I am of the nature to die. There is no way to escape death.

All that is dear to me and everyone I love are of the nature to change. There is no way to escape being separated from them.

My actions are my only true belongings. I cannot escape the consequences of my actions. My actions are the ground upon which I stand.

To these truths Jesus adds one more: I am a ceaseless being with an eternal destiny in God's great universe.

Surrender means giving up ultimate mastery of my life. However, I am not called to do this grudgingly. "A person may yield to a stronger person, or an army to a stronger army. One may yield to God because he is almighty. None of this is full surrender. Only if one experiences that God is good is it possible to surrender to him unconditionally one's whole heart, soul, and being."

Because I am creature and not Creator, surrender is actually a better way to play the game. For I am not Master of the Board. Surrender opens me up to God's blessing.

The Blessing of Wonder

One of the problems the illusion of being Master of the Board leads to is that by insisting I am smart enough to engineer my life, I close myself off to wonderful surprises. Often our efforts to control outcomes damage us worse than anything anyone else can do. Peter Drucker writes about the German scientist who synthesized novocaine, the first nonaddictive narcotic, in the early twentieth century. He intended for it to be used in major surgical procedures like amputations. But surgeons didn't like it; they preferred total anesthesia. Instead, novocaine became favored by dentists. (By the way—aren't you grateful to God for novocaine?)

One man was not grateful for this turn of events—its inventor! He spent the rest of his career traveling to dental schools giving talks that forbade dentists to use novocaine in ways he had not intended. He was not in control of how his invention got used—and it's lucky for us he was not! Imagine inventing novocaine, then trying to squelch its greatest use simply because that wasn't your little plan.

When I try to control something too tightly based on my own little ideas, I miss all the creativity and serendipity of life.

When I finished college, the highest-rated graduate school I applied to turned me down in the final round. At the time, I was frustrated and disappointed because my will had not been done. It wasn't until much later that I realized that had I gone there, I never would have gone to seminary, never would have worked at a church, never would have discovered what I came to understand to be my true calling. Today I would be working with lab rats. (Last but not least, I never would have met my wife or had my children.) How often when I insist on my own way I miss a way that is far better.

The Freedom to Love

A deeper problem with trying to be Master of the Board is that it puts me at odds with other people. When I live in the myth of control, other people are a problem. They do not behave the way I want them to, so I try to find some way to manipulate them, placate them, flatter them, intimidate them, or boss them around.

"And it came to pass there went out a decree from *me....*"

I walk into work: things are run my way, my projects have been completed, tasks I have assigned have been carried out. What does that mean? It means I'm in charge. This is my little kingdom.

I go into my kids' rooms: beds are made just as I prescribed, chores are done just as I commanded. What does that mean? It means I'm in charge. This is my little kingdom.

I walk through the door at the end of the day: my slippers are laid out by the La-Z-Boy, my iced tea is ready, my paper is waiting for me, my dinner is on the stove. What does that mean? It means I have walked into the wrong house.

We all get a little confused about whose kingdom it is. The drama team at Willow Creek Community Church used to do a sketch featuring a character named Pastor Howitzer. He was what General Patton might have been if Patton had gone into church work. He showed a visiting couple the organizational chart of the church. It looked like this:

ME

Everybody else

Recently, he said, they had done a reorganization of church leadership. The new organizational chart looked like this:

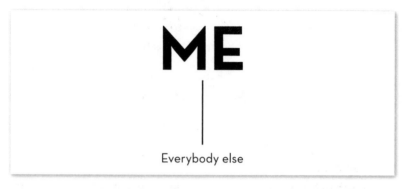

In every wedding there is a control freak, generally known as the "Mother of the Bride" (MOTB for short; just like Master of the Board). Given my occupation, I have seen a lot of them. I know of one church organist named Tom who, along with everyone else, was being driven crazy by a MOTB who was critiquing both his musical selections and keyboard style. Tom was an expert at a common form of organist humor — hiding well-known melodies in elaborate arrangements (for instance, weaving the theme from *Star Wars* into an old hymn). In this case, the MOTB beamed as she walked down the aisle to rapturous music; she would have beamed at a much lower wattage if she would have recognized it was a variation on "The Old Gray Mare." I remember one wedding where the MOTB was not happy with anything. She wanted a different shade of flowers in the church. The candles were too white. The music was too loud. She had a few suggestions for me too. She said if I didn't get a decent-looking pair of shoes, she would have me replaced.

And that was my wife's mother on the day of our wedding. (Actually, I'm immensely blessed to have a mother-in-law who is one of the most giving people I know.) But every one of us will have to come up against the hard truth that other people are not under our control.

Epictetus wrote, "If you think you have free rein over things that are naturally beyond your control, or if you attempt to adopt the affairs of others as your own, your purpose will be thwarted and you will become a frustrated, anxious, and fault-finding person."

Jesus taught concerning our relation-ships with other people, "Simply let your 'Yes' be 'Yes,' and your 'No,' 'No.'" He was not giving rules for what kind of oaths Christians are allowed to make. He was

> *Jesus taught that we should speak truth without using words to manipulate, intimidate, deceive, or flatter.*

saying that in our dealing with others we should simply speak truth and appeal to the free choice of others in a way that honors the dignity of their own kingdoms. We should speak truth without using words to manipulate, intimidate, deceive, or flatter.

With Surrender Comes Hope

As I write these words, the bestselling book in San Francisco is called *The Year of Magical Thinking*. As written by a gifted and successful author named Joan Didion, it is an attempt to make sense of the sud-den death of her equally gifted and successful author-husband, John Gregory Dunne. They had come home from the hospital where their only child was in a coma (she would die the following year). They sat down for dinner, and he died of a massive coronary. The book's title refers to her growing awareness that she kept behaving as if some-how her husband would come back: if she could just find out enough information about how he died; if she would not give away all of his clothes; if she would remain alone at night, he would return to her bed. She knew better, but she could not stop these irrational thoughts that death would not be allowed the last word.

Didion writes how people in her world shared a habit of mind usu-ally credited to the very successful:

> They believed absolutely in their own management skills. They believed absolutely in the power of the telephone numbers they had at their fingertips; the right doctor, the major donor; the

person who could facilitate a favor at State or Justice. The management skills of these people were in fact prodigious. I had myself for most of my life shared the same core belief in my ability to control events.

Yet ...

Some events just happen. This was one of those events. You sit down to dinner and life as you know it ends.

In the end, she concludes, we all are powerless. We live our lives above a frayed safety net. One of the lines that recurs in her book is a reaction to Jesus' teaching. I believe, she writes, that "no eye is on the sparrow." It is the last line in her book.

If I really am Master of the Board, my hopes die when I do. But if there is another Master, a better Master, then there is a better hope. A classic example of this comes from the biblical story of Joseph. Out of jealousy, his brothers sold him into slavery when he was seventeen. He spent many years in servitude and then in prison; yet in the end, the very attempts to destroy him led to his becoming the most powerful man in Egypt next to Pharaoh. When Joseph's brothers realized his great power, they threw themselves before him, saying, "We are your slaves."

But Joseph didn't want slaves. He had come to realize that there is a Great Power at work in the world. "Don't be afraid. Am I in the place of God? You intended to harm me, but God intended it for good to accomplish what is now being done, the saving of many lives," he said. Why did it "come to pass" that Joseph was a slave, and then a prisoner, and then a ruler? Someone's eye was on the sparrow.

With Surrender Comes Power

Jesus taught many times about this strange truth that power comes to us not when we seek control but when we freely yield our little centers of control to God. He said that if a grain of wheat remains alone, it bears no fruit, but if it is placed in the ground and dies, then it lives. He said that if we deny ourselves, we are fulfilled. He said that if we seek to save our lives, we lose them, but when we lose them for his sake, we come alive.

In all of these expressions, we are actually receiving greater power by surrendering. For instance, take alcoholism and sobriety. One of the great discoveries of Alcoholics Anonymous is that if an alcoholic tries to control her drinking through willpower, she is condemned to failure. There is only so much that willpower can accomplish.

> *We actually receive greater power by surrendering.... There is only so much that willpower can accomplish.*

However, sobriety is possible. The first step toward it is for the alcoholic to acknowledge the limitations of her own control. ("We acknowledged we were powerless to control our drinking.") The next step is to place her dependence in the hands of another source, a higher power. Then, the alcoholic must humble herself by engaging in other activities — taking a ruthless moral inventory, seeking to atone for past wrongs, engaging in fellowship, and helping others. And then, through the process known as the twelve steps, the alcoholic *receives* the power to do what she could not do on her own.

Freedom from Anxiety over Outcomes

Some time ago a guest speaker named Richie Cunningham came to our church. (It wasn't really Richie Cunningham; it was actually Dallas Willard, but I get tired of quoting him all the time.) He had spoken at a Q-and-A session for several hundred of our leaders, and afterward we were walking to the car to go to another event where he would speak. I noticed how relaxed he was and that he was humming an old hymn.

It struck me that when most people finish speaking (including me), their immediate thoughts cluster around questions such as "How do you think it went?" "Did I do well?" "Do you think people liked it?" Many times the service is hardly over before those who put it on are asking themselves if it was successful.

If indicators are that a speaking opportunity went well, then I feel buoyed up. I feel somehow validated as a person. I have a tiny little piece of celebrity to rejoice over. I have a little extra energy; I would be happy to stick around after it's over and talk to people. Maybe I will do a double lap around the parking lot just in case anybody's still hanging out to tell me it went well.

On the other hand, if I think it went poorly, I feel deflated. I wonder if perhaps I have lost my fastball. I wonder how many people noticed how badly I did. I want to hide. Either way, I can find myself obsessing about the outcome, replaying it over in my mind, thinking of how it might have gone differently.

But what I noticed in Richie Cunningham was this tremendous sense of freedom. His worth as a person was not on the line. He had genuinely tried to be helpful to people while he was speaking. And when he was done—he was done. He was not worried about what other people thought of *him*. He could finish what he was doing and simply let go of it like a child releasing a helium balloon into the atmosphere. The outcome was not a referendum on him; it was in someone else's hands entirely.

I would love that kind of freedom. I realized watching him that trusting God means learning to let go of each moment so I am free to fully inhabit the next one. There is simply no call for me to try to control people or outcomes. Someone far better is already on that job.

That is why I can never get control issues right apart from partnership with God. I must come to trust that he actually is looking out for me and is perfectly competent to oversee the cosmos. I remember the little words that remind Caesar, Yertle, and me who is really Master of the Board: "And it came to pass...."

CHAPTER 7

No One Else
Can Take Your Turn

Everyone must carry two pieces of paper with him
and look at them every day. On one it is written:
"You are as dust and ashes." And on the other:
"For you the universe was created."

RABBINIC SAYING

My dad and I were in the semifinals of what was for us a big tournament. We were playing against a doubles team that was better than us, one we had never come close to beating. I would have sold my grandmother to beat this team. We were in a third set tiebreaker, and in that era it was a nine-point, first-team-to-five affair. The score reached four-all. One point would be sudden death. It's harder than it sounds.

I was serving. My first serves had been going okay, but my second serves had been shaky all match long — a lethal combination of slowness and inconsistency. I was serving to an opponent who ate weak second serves with buttered toast for breakfast. I went for an ace on my first serve, and would have had one if it hadn't been out by ten feet or so.

As I stood on the baseline nervously bouncing the ball, I reflected on philosopher Bernard Suits's thesis in his article "What Is a Game?" A game is at its heart the creation of a challenge against which one tests oneself. What makes a game good, he argues, is that it embodies well-crafted problems. And it is in the owning and embracing of the problem that players are able to grow in what the Greek Olympians called *arête*: excellence of will and character. It was at this point I recognized a major flaw in tennis: there was no bull pen, no relief pitcher, no substitute, no place to hide. I wanted a designated server. In tennis *no one else can take your turn.*

(You may be wondering whatever happened to my second serve. I hope you love mystery.)

You are not a pawn, a victim of circumstances beyond your control. Instead, you are responsible for your own life. No one else can take your turn. There are no designated hitters. You are not allowed to say, "Pass."

You have a "turn" every time you have an opportunity to choose. But most of us see only a tiny fraction of the choices we have. One of the best exercises for playing the game wisely is to be conscious of making decisions. The more you become aware of how many choices are up to you, the more eagerly you embrace your turn. You can practice this today. What will you feed your mind? What thoughts will you dwell on? Whom will you have conversations with? Where will you direct your desires? How will you take care of your body? What acts of service will you engage in? When will you choose to be interrupted, and when will you choose to stay on task? What will you eat? How will you spend your time? All of these are calls you will make, and when you add them up, they create your life. No one else can take your turn.

One of the champions of making wise choices in the Bible is Daniel. The first seven verses of the book named for him tell the story of a man who was a victim of circumstances far beyond his control. King Nebuchadnezzar conquered his land and carried him into exile in Babylon. Daniel lost his freedom, his home, his culture, his friendships, and his status as one of Israel's nobility. He had to learn to speak a foreign language and live and die in a place he never wanted to be. He even lost his name. His Hebrew name, Daniel, meant "the Lord will judge."

But he was not Daniel anymore. He was given a Babylonian name, Belteshazzar, as a not-so-subtle reminder that he was not even in control of his own identity anymore. If I had been Daniel, I would have been tempted to spend my time and energy focused on things I could not control: complaining about what a bad leader Nebuchadnezzar was, blaming the exile for my unhappiness, feeling sorry for myself, critiquing reality to anyone who would listen.

But Daniel didn't do this. In the beginning of the story, it's the Babylonians who have determined everything: Nebuchadnezzar determined to conquer Israel, determined to cart off its most sacred objects and its highest potential citizens, determined to enroll them in his leadership academy, and determined the entrance criteria and subject matter.

Then in Daniel 1:8 the initiative shifts: "But *Daniel* determined that he would not defile himself by eating the king's food or drinking his wine." It is a strong word reserved for a firm decision: "he resolved in his heart" that he would honor God. He would take his turn. He spent time thinking about what he most deeply valued and desired. He strategized. He was realistic about obstacles. He empathized with the dean of the school and found a solution that could appeal to him as well.

Daniel went to the dean of the school to talk about the menu. He explained that everyone was being fed roast beef, eggs, and cheese, but he wanted to be on the Jerusalem diet. The text doesn't say why the food would defile Daniel—maybe it was in violation of ceremonial law; maybe it had been offered to idols. The writer is less interested in dietary details than this: Daniel *chose.*

When you find yourself floating in a sea of helplessness, you must find some concrete way to express your freely embraced deepest commitment. Daniel acted. He found a concrete way to reclaim his initiative and personhood.

> *When you are floating in a sea of helplessness, you must find some concrete way to express your freely embraced deepest commitment.*

Daniel's actions took enormous courage. Nebuchadnezzar was not the kind of leader who cut people a lot of slack. Once a puppet king named Zedekiah rebelled against him. Nebuchadnezzar had Zedekiah's sons killed before his eyes and then had his eyes cut out. You have heard of leaders with "hands-on" or "hands-off" management styles. Nebuchadnezzar had a "heads-off" management style. When people crossed him, he cut off their heads. Your boss may be tough. But when Nebuchadnezzar terminated people, he *terminated* people.

The dean of the school was reluctant. He told Daniel that if he agreed to let Daniel not eat the royal diet, Daniel might get emaciated, and the king would have the dean's head. At that point we see Daniel's persistence and street smarts. He said to himself, *That was not exactly a yes, but not exactly a no either.*

He went to the guard and proposed an experiment. He said, "Let's try this diet for ten days, and you be the judge." Imagine what those ten days were like for everyone involved. For ten days Daniel's future hung in the balance. Daniel exercised amazing initiative, courage, moxie, and faith that God would work.

And God did! "*Now God* had caused the official to show favor and sympathy to Daniel," the text says. Daniel did not know ahead of time *how* things would work out, but he was not operating alone. Sometimes we shrink back from resolving in our hearts because we don't know how things will work out. But we forget the "Now God" factor. Daniel did so well that the guard took away everybody's steak and put the whole school on the veggie platter. And Daniel went to the head of the class and was named valedictorian.

As they went through life, Daniel and his friends would have to make some very difficult decisions. When they were told to bow down and worship the king or be thrown into the furnace, they said, "Throw us into the furnace — we will not bow." When Daniel was told, "Cease praying to your god or you'll be thrown to the lions," he said, "Throw me to the lions, for I will not stop praying."

If he and his friends had not taken action early on, if they had not declared to the world and themselves where their deepest allegiance belonged, they never would have had the strength to face the furnace and the lions' den.

A Study in Contrast

There's a great guy I like to spend time with. Externally he has faced nowhere near the challenges Daniel did, but internally he's much unhappier about his life. He's significantly discontented with his work. He feels he should be given a much more stretching and demanding job. He's convinced that his supervisor will not recognize his potential, and he won't develop his gifts. He talks about how the organization where he works is too political for him to get promoted.

"What if you were to take another job?" I ask him. "Why don't you look at some other companies? Why don't you go ahead and apply for a promotion or a transfer somewhere else? Why don't you go back to school for more education?"

No. Taking another job might be too risky. Transferring to another department would just bring more of the same—politics are everywhere. Education would be a waste of time; he's too old. He has these grandiose dreams for what he should be doing, but he won't take just one step at a time from where he is.

This guy wants to be in a romantic relationship. He develops crushes on women from a distance. They are more or less in the supermodel category, and he is not in that category. He won't form a realistic relationship. He will occasionally have a polite conversation with the woman du jour, and he will dream about the possibility of a relationship, but it never goes anywhere.

I suggest a good counselor who could help him work on these problems. That would cost too much money he says.

"Could I help out?" I ask.

Well, it would also take up too much time.

"I'll bet if we went through your calendar together we could find some time."

Well, that kind of stuff never really helps anyway. Counselors just don't understand him.

He doesn't like his life. Sometimes he blames God for it, as if God has done this to him. Sometimes—for I know him well—I take him by the lapels. "This is your one and only life; you're throwing it away a year at a time. You don't have to," I say. I want to put my hands around his neck and choke some sense into him. This is why in psychology graduate school my supervisor encouraged me to look for another line of work.

> *He is living as if he were a pawn. He is waiting for something to happen outside of him to change his circumstances and make him happy.*

He is living as if he were a pawn. He is waiting for something to happen outside of him to change his circumstances and make him happy. Every time his turn comes up, he gives the same response: "Pass."

Sometimes people ask me, "How can I become a writer?" I tell them how it usually works: Write an article. Submit it to a journal. Get rejected. Submit it some more. Get rejected some more. Write another one. Submit it. Get rejected again. Learn how to edit. Get an article accepted. Repeat the process about a hundred times. Get asked to write a few chapters in a book for someone. Cowrite a book with somebody else. Keep learning.

Sometimes I will get this response: "No, I don't want to go that route. I've already written a book. I just need to find the publisher who will take it and sell more copies than *The Da Vinci Code* and *Harry Potter* put together."

Good luck with that.

Why Taking Your Turn Matters

There is a reason why you must take your turn—or die. God has given to you a tiny measure of what he has without limit—the ability to choose. Psychologists use words like *initiative* or *being proactive* or *taking responsibility*. But these are not just psychological concepts. They are deeply connected to what it means to be made in the image of God.

"Then God said, 'Let us make human beings in our image, in our likeness ... and let them have *dominion....*'" Dominion is a kingdom word. God's plan is that "everybody gets a turn."

What is a two-year-old's favorite word? *No!* Two-year-olds are learning what it means to have a kingdom. Little kids in the backseat of a car draw a line. "You'd better not cross over." They are staking out their kingdoms back there. Then they start defending their kingdoms.

Dad turns around (whose kingdom does Dad think the car is?): "Do you want me to come back there?"

The kids think to themselves, *Sure—you're gonna come back while the car is going seventy down the expressway.*

Dad sends Mr. Hand back like a snake. The kids, being no fools, retreat to neutral corners. Christian humorist Ken Davis gives advice on how to get them out of the unreachable safety zone: "A tap on the brakes brings them right into play."

"Thy kingdom come."

Having a kingdom is a very good thing. It's part of what God made you for—to be a powerful and creative force for good in the world. When our sense of dominion dies—when we feel like we have no control over our lives—then we die as well.

Losing Our Turn

One of the most devastating experiences in life is a sense that what I do does not matter. Perhaps the most important research into depression over the last many decades was a series of experiments that showed it is brought on by a sense of "learned helplessness." Experimenters gave groups of dogs a series of small electric shocks. Some dogs learned they could stop the shocks by jumping over a wall; other dogs were given shocks at random. The second group simply lay down and quit trying to do anything. Later on they were put in the setting where they could have stopped the shocks by jumping over the wall, but they never tried. They "learned" that they were helpless.

Human beings are even more vulnerable to learned helplessness, as performance psychologist James Loeher points out.

In concentration camps or prisoner of war environments, the greatest difference between people who give up and people who remain resilient is a sense that they can still control something, according to psychologist Julius Segal. In nursing homes, such trivial choices as getting to decide when to see a movie or how to arrange their rooms made seniors' health and emotional well-being improve and the death rate drop. Daniel flourished because even in exile he refused to believe he was helpless.

Where Do I Have a Choice?

Epictetus was a Greek philosopher whose circumstances fluctuated wildly. Like Daniel, he lived much of his life in captivity. He was born a slave; his brilliance earned him an education in Rome; the power and influence of his teaching caused some emperors to make him their teacher and others to see him as a threat; he ended his life living in a hovel and dying in exile. All this, he said, was out of his control and therefore not to be worried over. "Within our control are our own opinions, aspirations, desires, and the things that repel us. These areas are quite rightly our concern because they are directly subject to our influence. We always have a choice about the contents and character of our inner lives."

We will all, like Daniel, spend some time in Babylon. Sometimes dreams will go unfulfilled, health will disappear, hopes will fade. The key question is never, "What have I lost?" It is "What do I have left? Where can I still take my turn?"

David Rabin was a professor of medicine at Vanderbilt University. While going through medical school, the disease that he found most frightening was amyotrophic lateral sclerosis, or Lou Gehrig's disease. He remembered being introduced to his first patient with the disease, hearing the neurologist announce, "Hopeless! He will be demeaned, isolated, unable to communicate, and probably dead in six months."

When he was forty-six, Rabin was himself diagnosed with ALS. He knew what would happen: stiffness in the legs, then weakness;

paralysis of the lower limbs and then the upper; eventually he became trapped in a body that would no longer obey his commands. His tongue lost its ability to function; he could form words only with the greatest of difficulty, and eventually not at all.

He lost his ability to treat patients. He could no longer go to the hospital to work. He would have had a brilliant academic career; now he could no longer turn the pages of a book.

> *The key question is never, "What have I lost?" It is "What do I have left? Where can I still take my turn?"*

But there was one thing he would not surrender: he would not surrender his spirit. He heard from a fellow physician who also had ALS about a computer that could be operated by a single switch. That switch could be operated by anyone—however handicapped—who retained the function of one muscle group.

David had enough strength in only one part of his body—his eyebrow muscle. And so for the next four years he used his eyebrow. With his eyebrow he could operate a computer. So with his eyebrow he could speak to his family, tell jokes to his friends, write papers, and review manuscripts. He carried on a medical consulting practice. He taught med students. He published a comprehensive textbook on endocrinology and received a prestigious award for his work. And he did all this when the only thing he could control was a single eyebrow. He said, "Sickness may challenge your body. But are you merely your body? Lameness may impede your legs. But you are not merely your legs. Your will is bigger than your legs. For your will is always under your own control."

Here was a man whose body would not win any competitions or grace any magazine covers. It was twisted, useless, helpless, and hopeless. But it housed two assets: an eyebrow muscle strong enough to twitch on command and a spirit that would not give up. And one eyebrow was enough to serve the world.

Got a good eyebrow? Then it's your turn.

Your body is not you. Your job is not you. Your success, reputation, and possessions are not you. What your parents, boss, peers, friends, or enemies think of you is not you. Your circumstances and limitations are not you. Psychologist Dan Baker puts it like this: "There is a *you* in you nobody put there."

The Ultimate Freedom

Viktor Frankl was a highly respected psychiatrist in Vienna who lost everything when the Nazis rose to power. They took his home, career, and freedom. His parents, brother, and wife—his entire family except for his sister—were killed in the gas ovens. Frankl spent years in Auschwitz where he was beaten, starved, brutalized, and dehumanized; where he saw his companions die daily. The manuscript he had devoted his life to, pinned all his scholarly hopes on, was found and destroyed.

The suffering and torture inflicted on Frankl are difficult to absorb. Made to compete with other prisoners for scraps of food. Made to work in the snow with no shoes. Forced to watch the random execution of friends at the whim of a guard. Never knowing from one day to the next if he would be forced to shovel out the ashes that had the day before been his friends' bodies or if he would be part of the ashes.

Gradually, emaciated, naked, humiliated, sick, without reasonable hope of liberation or reunion with loved ones, Frankl began to realize that there was one freedom left to him. He saw how some prisoners, even though they were starving, would offer their bread to others. He saw how some prisoners, though weakened, tried to comfort those even weaker. He came to realize "everything can be taken from a man but one thing: the last of the human freedoms—to choose one's attitude in any given set of circumstances, to choose one's own way."

There, in that camp, Frankl began to make decisions. He chose to cherish the thought of those he loved. He chose to give what help as a doctor he was able to offer to others.

He looked for ways to exercise this freedom. He grew very conscious about making choices: choosing what he would think about, what memories he would dwell on, what words he would speak, how he would say them, what help he would offer, how he would respond to humiliation, how he would walk, how he would hold his head high.

And Frankl's freedom began to expand. One writer puts it like this: his guards had more *liberty*—they could leave the camp, walk where they chose, spend what they wanted. But Frankl had more *freedom*.

Now It's Your Turn

Once more: one of the best exercises for playing the game wisely is to be conscious of making decisions.

There is an old hymn we sang in the church where I grew up:

> *Dare to be a Daniel,*
> *Dare to stand alone!*
> *Dare to have purpose firm!*
> *Dare to make it known.*

So take the next ten days to go on a Daniel adventure. Pick some area where you can take action. And for ten days, choose to honor God in that area. Maybe, like Daniel, it will involve what you eat. Or maybe it will concern what you choose to feed your mind. Maybe you will seek to go ten days without complaining to anyone. Maybe each day for the next ten days you will choose to read the book of Daniel.

Perhaps for the next ten days what will help you take your turn is to become intensely aware of all the deci-

Never give up your spirit.
Take action.
Find meaning in suffering.

sions that are open to you. Some of them are absurdly small: you can sleep on the opposite side of the bed! You can brush your teeth *before* breakfast. You can choose what you will wear, how you comb your hair, what you read, what you listen to, who you call on the phone, what notes you write, what music you listen to, what route you take to work, what time you get up on Saturday. Some of them will be larger. You can refuse to allow your boss or spouse the power to dictate what kind of mood you will be in through the day based on how he or she treats you. Like Daniel, you can choose.

Never give up your spirit. Never yield emotionally.

Take action. Do something—even if you're not sure what. Taking action helps prevent sinking into helplessness.

Find meaning in suffering. Maybe through your suffering you will be able to help someone else; maybe you will be able to grow stronger; maybe the meaning simply is a conviction that God will be able to bring good out of it that you cannot now see.

Remember Daniel and the "Now God" factor. When you resolve in your heart to honor God, he becomes involved in your life in ways you cannot foresee.

It's your turn now.

CHAPTER 8

REMEMBER YOUR STUFF ISN'T YOURS

I go around doing nothing
but persuading both young and old
not to care for your body or your wealth
in preference to your soul.

SOCRATES

It's only stuff.

We all have stuff. We see it, want it, buy it, display it, insure it, and compare it with other people's stuff. We talk about whether or not they have too much stuff; we envy or pass judgment on other people's collections of stuff. We collect our own little pile. We imagine that if that pile got big enough, we would feel successful or secure.

That's how you keep score in Monopoly, and that's how our culture generally keeps score as well.

You get a house, then you have to get stuff to put in it. You keep getting more stuff, and you need a bigger house. A house, said comedian George Carlin, is just a pile of stuff with a cover on it. Some people have actually survived without owning one. Jesus, for instance.

There are now more than 30,000 self-storage facilities in the country offering over a billion square feet for people to store their stuff. In the 1960s, this industry did not exist. We now spend $12 billion a year just to pay someone to store our extra stuff! It's larger than the music industry.

Psychologist Paul Pearsall comments on people finding it difficult to give their stuff away:

Many people can't bring themselves to get rid of any of their stuff.

You may require a "closet exorcist." A trusted friend can help prevent the "re-stuffing phenomenon." Re-stuff happens when, in the process of cleaning out closets and drawers, we are somehow stimulated to acquire new stuff. Beware of the stuff co-addicts, who may see a closet cleaning as a chance to acquire stuff for themselves from your stuff supply. Such friends are likely to go with you on a re-stuffing expedition.

Some people have a gift for acquiring stuff. Not long ago I took my daughter to a place called Hearst Castle. William Randolph Hearst was a "stuffaholic." He had 3,500-year-old Egyptian statues, medieval Flemish tapestries, and centuries-old hand-carved ceilings, and some of the greatest works of art of all time, most of which came from Sweden.

He built a house of 72,000 square feet to put his stuff in. He acquired property for his house: 265,000 acres; he originally owned fifty miles of California coastline. He collected stuff for eighty-eight years. Then you know what he did?

He died. That was shortsighted.

Now people go through Hearst's house by the thousands. They all say the same thing: "Wow, he sure had a lot of stuff."

People go through life, get stuff, and then they die, leaving all their stuff behind. What happens to it? The kids argue over it. The kids—who haven't died yet, who are really just pre-dead people—go over to their parents' house. They pick through their parents' old stuff like vultures, deciding which stuff they want to take to their houses. They say to themselves, "Now this is my stuff." Then they die—and some new vultures come for it. People come and go. Nations go to war over stuff, families are split apart because of stuff. Husbands and wives argue more about stuff than any other single issue.

Prisons are full of street thugs and CEOs who committed crimes to acquire it.

Why? It's only stuff. Houses and hotels are the crowning jewels in Monopoly. But the moment the game ends they go back in the box. So it is with all our stuff.

Stuff Is Not Treasure

Jesus said, "Do not store up for yourselves treasures on earth, where moth and rust destroy, and where thieves break in and steal. But store up for yourselves treasures in heaven, where moth and rust do not destroy, and where thieves do not break in and steal. For where your treasure is, there your heart will be also."

Let's say you spend a week at Motel 6. How likely would it be for you to take all your money and spend it decorating your motel room? How probable is it that you would clean out your bank account to purchase van Goghs or paintings of Elvis on velvet or whatever it is that your taste runs to?

Not very. You wouldn't even be tempted, because the motel room is *not home*. You're only going to be there a little while. It would be foolish to waste the treasure of your one and only life on a temporary residence.

Smart players are clear on what lasts and what doesn't. So Jesus says it is wise to store up treasure in what's eternal: God and people.

This is Motel 6. Your "room" — your home and furniture and clothes and possessions — will last the equivalent of a few seconds compared to the eternity that will be occupied by your soul. It's not bad to stay in a place and enjoy it while you're there. But Jesus says don't store up treasure in Motel 6. It's not home. You're only going to be here a little while. If you're going to stay up nights dreaming, dream about something better than how to upgrade your motel room.

> *Smart players are clear on what lasts and what doesn't. It is wise to store up treasure in what's eternal: God and people.*

Stuff Cannot Belong to Me

To an adult, it's ironic when a two-year-old says, "Mine."

Adults know that two-year-olds don't earn any of their stuff. It is all provided for them. It is a gift from someone much larger and wiser than they. They don't even generally take very good care of it.

Nevertheless, two-year-olds get extremely attached to their stuff. If someone tries to take something, that item suddenly becomes their favorite stuff. Two-year-olds can be so deluded, can't they?

Consider a few statements from Scripture: "The earth is the LORD's, and everything in it, the world, and all who live in it." "Remember the LORD your God, for it is he who gives you the ability to produce wealth." "'The silver is mine and the gold is mine,' declares the LORD Almighty."

I have been around churches for a long time. Do you know what the most frequently asked question about tithing is? "Do I have to tithe on the net or on the gross?" Translation: "How little can I give and not get God mad at me?" The implied question is: "How much of *my stuff* can I keep and not get in trouble?" This is like going to your mom on Mother's Day and saying, "Mom, what's the least amount of money I can spend on your present without severing our relationship?"

King David once said to God, "But who am I, and who are my people, that we should be able to give as generously as this?" He doesn't ask, "What's the least amount I have to give and not get God ticked off?" He says, "Who am I, that I should be able to give like this? I want to use my stuff to build *your* kingdom, not *my* kingdom."

One day we will give an account for what God has entrusted to us. That can be an occasion of great joy or of deep regret. Some time ago we borrowed a friend's car. We had a two-car garage that was full; our friend's car was sitting in the driveway. We have five drivers in our family; three of them are teenagers. Somebody got into a car in the garage and backed out without checking the rearview mirror. *Boom!* I don't want to tell you who it was because I don't want to embarrass that person. It was not, however, one of the teenage drivers. Nor was it my wife. What a bad feeling I had when it was time to return the car: "Here's what you entrusted to me. I didn't do real well with it. I had an accident—in the driveway."

It's not my stuff. And one day I will give account.

One of the most amazing statements about the early church is that "there were no needy persons among them." If they had stuff, they shared it. There had never been a community like this.

Stuff Cannot Last

Speaker Randy Alcorn sometimes invites his listeners to go for an imaginary ride. We're in line behind a few dozen pickups. They are filled with old furniture and rusted refrigerators and obsolete TV sets and velvet pictures of Elvis. One by one they stop at the top of a hill; the drivers get out and throw the stuff from their trucks over the edge of the hill to whatever's below.

You get out of your car to look over the edge and see what's going on. You see nothing but acres and acres of junk. It is Old Stuff Home. It used to be called a junkyard or a dump, but nobody wants to live next to one of those, so now we call it a "landfill." *Garbage* and *dump* and *junk* are sad words, but filling up land with more land sounds positive. Who doesn't want the world to have more land?

It's a dump all the same, and that's where old stuff goes to die. Flat screen TVs and sub-zero refrigerators (they don't actually get that cold; "subzero" refers to your IQ at the mo-

> *It's not that such treasures are bad. It's that they won't last. It's all going back in the box.*

ment you're willing to pay for an overpriced refrigerator) and toasters and Twinkies and pieces of old Lear jets will rot next to each other in the democracy of decay. It's not that such treasures are *bad*. It's that they won't last. Stuff is a foolish investment. It's all going back in the box.

Stuff Cannot Make You Free

Paul says, "Those who want to get rich fall into temptation and a trap and into many foolish and harmful desires that plunge people into ruin and destruction." Not having stuff can lead you into the trap. Ironically, getting more doesn't lead to more freedom. Getting can be its own trap. Randy Alcorn notes the comments of some of the wealthiest people of their day:

> *"The care of $200 million is enough to kill anyone.*
> *There is no pleasure in it."*
> **W. H. Vanderbilt**
>
> *"I am the most miserable man on earth."*
> **J. J. Astor**
>
> *"I have made millions,*
> *but they have brought me no happiness."*
> **John D. Rockefeller**
>
> *"Millionaires seldom smile."*
> **Andrew Carnegie**
>
> *"I was happier when doing a mechanic's job."*
> **Henry Ford**

Stuff Cannot Make Me Happy

We are desiring creatures. We can't stop desiring any more than we can stop breathing. But we can decide what sights and messages we will expose our minds to, and these in turn will shape our desires. By the mid-1970s, Americans were spending more time in shopping malls than any places other than work and home.

Ever get any mail-order catalogs delivered to your house? Take a guess at the total number of mail-order catalogs that get sent out in this country per year.

The correct answer: Forty billion (that's right—*billion*!).

And every one of them is designed with the same objective: to make you desire more. They are in the "need-creating" business. Things that we used to put in the "want" category keep getting shifted into the "need" category, and we feel we can't get along without them. We suffer from "catalog-induced anxiety." Here's the problem: you cannot get enough of what you do not need.

You can get more. But as we will see in a later chapter, it will never be enough.

Stuff Cannot Make Me Secure

This is perhaps where the teaching of Jesus and his followers most radically diverges from conventional wisdom. Paul said, "We brought nothing into the world, and we can take nothing out of it." Job said, "Naked I came from my mother's womb, and naked I will depart."

We come in naked and penniless; we're going out naked and penniless. In between we get some stuff to put on our bodies and some stuff in our pockets, but none of it is really ours. We borrow it for a while; then one day we will hand it all back in.

My desire for financial security discourages me from giving. Each dollar I give away is no longer available for my protection. But my sense of freedom always *increases* when I give because giving is a declaration that my security rests someplace other than the bank. Giving is an act of confidence in God.

Stuff Can Help Me Become Rich toward God

Jon Haidt is a University of Virginia professor who found himself worn down by the study of human pathology. He began to explore that which elevates the human spirit to try to find out what creates lasting joy. He calls such emotion "elevation." A freshman coed relates a typical story:

We were going home from working at the Salvation Army shelter on a snowy night. We passed an old woman shoveling her driveway. One of the guys asked the driver to let him out. I thought he was just going to take a shortcut home. But when I saw him pick up the shovel, well, I felt a lump in my throat and started to cry. I wanted to tell everyone about it. I felt romantic toward him.

A fellow psychology professor, Martin Seligman, engaged his class in a debate about whether happiness comes more readily from acts of kindness or from having fun. He gave them a unique assignment: engage in one philanthropic activity and one pleasurable activity and write about both. "The results were life-changing. The afterglow of the pleasurable activity (hanging out with friends, or watching a movie, or eating a hot fudge sundae) paled with the effects of the kind action. When our philanthropic acts were spontaneous and called upon personal strengths, the whole day went better."

Early on in our marriage, I taught a class at a seminary and got paid for it. In those days we had very little money, so I set a financial goal: I decided that within a year I would surprise my wife by kidnapping her for a weekend and giving her a new wedding ring. (The one I gave to her at our wedding had a diamond in it, but it was only visible through a microscope. It was a step below the rings you get in a box of Cracker Jacks.) For the next twelve months, I socked away every check I got for doing weddings and funerals. I was secretive to the point of deception with her about money: "No, I guess I won't get paid for that wedding either."

When the weekend finally came, I had arranged for the kids to stay with my parents. I took her to the airport, and we flew to the coast to stay in a fabulous hotel. I had her ring hidden by a waiter in a cherry tomato in her salad. And I found that as much joy as she got out of the weekend, I got even more. The thought occurred to me, as I watched her mouth drop open when she saw the ring in her tomato, *It's really true, what Jesus said. It really is better to give. Giving is the best!*

When we give casually, we receive casual joy. When we give effortfully, thoughtfully, creatively, we get immense joy. In the Old Testament, David was once offered everything he needed to give an offering to God. He turned it down, saying, "Shall I give to the Lord that which costs me nothing?" David understood how satisfaction comes to the human heart.

> *When we give casually, we receive casual joy. When we give effortfully, thoughtfully, creatively, we get immense joy.*

Nancy has a cousin named Kenny who more or less doubled as her best friend when she was growing up. When I first met Kenny, he was a professional baseball player, a pitcher who could throw a baseball as if it were coming out of a cannon.

Kenny hurt his arm and never did end up in the major leagues. He always loved baseball. When our son was playing on a team in the fourth grade, he got a few stints as a pitcher. Uncle Kenny came out to watch him and afterward explained to Johnny how to throw a bean ball, which fortunately Johnny never used in game conditions.

Kenny ended up living in the South in a community where most people struggle pretty hard to make ends meet. He has a relative by marriage who was extremely ill and facing death unless someone donated a kidney. None of the biological relatives was a good match. But Kenny found out that he was compatible and donated one of his kidneys. That one gift has created so much joy and gratitude in both the giver and the receiver that the spiritual transaction was greater than the physical. If you were to ask Kenny what in his life he is most proud of, I suppose it would be the giving of that gift.

Richness of Having vs. Richness of Being

Yale theologian Miroslav Volf says that there are two kinds of richness in life: "richness of having" and "richness of being." Richness of having is an external circumstance. Richness of being is an inner experience. We usually focus on richness of having. We think true happiness lies there. Our language reflects this when the "haves" keep popping up in our thoughts:

If only I could have my dream house …
If only I could have a higher salary …
When I have a better car …
When I have enough money for the ultimate vacation …
If only I could have financial security/nicer clothes/better vacations/
    shinier toys …

We seek richness of having, but what we really want is richness of being. We want to be grateful, joyful, content, free from anxiety, and generous. We scramble after richness of having because we think it will produce richness of being, but it does not.

In the sense of "having," we can become rich by long hours, shrewd investments, and a lot of luck. But it is possible to *have* a barn full of money and a boatload of talent and movie star good looks and still *be* poor. The bottomless pit of our desires will never be satisfied. No matter how much we have, we remain what Volf calls "not-enough people." For not-enough people, there exists no lasting soul satisfaction. I saw an ad this week that featured the tagline "Yesterday I didn't know it existed; today I can't live without it." That is the disease of the not-enough soul.

On the other hand, we can *have* very little and yet *be* rich. A rich soul experiences life differently. It experiences a sense of *gratitude* for what it has received, rather than resentment for what it hasn't gotten. It faces the future with hope rather than anxiety. The apostle Paul discovered that when he was living as a friend and companion of Jesus, who "though he was rich, yet for [our] sakes he became poor." Paul himself experienced richness of being. He became a "more-than-enough" person. He found that whether he was living in luxury or living in prison he had more than enough, because he had been freed from the treadmill of *having*.

Richness of being is always available. I can seek at any time, with God's help, to be compassionate, generous, grateful, and joyful. And stuff can aid me in this. But usually it will not mean seeking to accumulate more stuff. Richness of having usually means getting more stuff; richness of being is generally associated with giving more stuff. Jesus' goal of "richness toward God" always involves richness of being.

> *Jesus' goal of "richness toward God" always involves richness of being.*

When I think of being rich and having riches, I think of two men. One of the men was part of a ministry for twentysomethings that my wife used to lead at Willow Creek Community Church. It is not a group that thinks much about death. When you are that age, you think you are going to live forever. I used to tease her that to draw a lot of people, she only had to teach on three subjects: sex, the end times, and will there be sex in the end times?

Then Larry Clarke died. Larry and I had gone to the same college. When he was in his thirties he quit his job so that he could serve full-time at the church (for no pay). He never married, never owned a home, never went on an expensive vacation. He just befriended people. He saw potential. He invited people into groups, into opportunities to make friends and contribute. He saw potential in discouraged people. He had radar for lonely people. He told people what he thought they could become.

Not long after Nancy had taken over the ministry, Larry, while at a leadership retreat in Milwaukee, was jogging downtown early in the morning and stepped in front of a bus and was struck and killed. His loss was devastating to that group of leaders, but even they had no idea of his impact.

A wake was held for Larry in the chapel of the church that week. No one was sure how many people would come: after all, Larry never married and had no children and no regular job. Cars came flooding in. The wake lasted three hours. So many people came to file past the casket that the line went out the chapel door for blocks; eight hundred people stood in line for three hours to honor him.

The next day was the funeral service. The chapel at Willow Creek can hold around five hundred people when jammed full. Over the decade or so that we served there, many funerals were held in the chapel, several of them for people of significant stature and achievement. Only one drew so many people that it overflowed the chapel and had to be moved to the main auditorium: Larry Clarke's.

At the service and the wake, at the reception and in the halls, one person after another spoke of how his or her life had been touched by Larry. None of the stories were about Larry's possessions or achievements. All of them were about Larry's capacity to love. We used to wonder how Larry could afford to give all his time away. Somebody at his funeral mentioned they heard Larry say one time that you'd be surprised how much good food you could find foraging behind Ralph's Supermarket that gets thrown out even though it is still packaged and fresh.

That same decade, a funeral was held for a man named Armand Hammer. At the age of ninety-two, Hammer was chairman of Occidental Petroleum Company. A billionaire industrialist and philanthropist, he was called by *USA Today* a "giant of capitalism and confidante of world leaders." It wasn't until his death that his story came out. Harvard-educated political scientist Edward Epstein wrote *Dossier: The Secret History of Armand Hammer,* in which he reported that Hammer got his start by laundering money for the Soviet government, then hired ghostwriters to write fictitious autobiographies of his life. He got more money through a string of broken marriages. He allowed his father to go to prison for a botched abortion Hammer himself had performed. He neglected his only son and hid himself from an illegitimate daughter. He had no friends at Occidental where "he fired his top executives as though they were errand boys." When his brother Victor died, he filed a claim of $667,000 against the $700,000 estate rather than disbursing it to Victor's children and nursing home–bound wife.

When Hammer died, his son Julian did not attend the funeral. Neither did the members of his two brothers' families. And neither did almost anyone else. Within days of his death, Occidental distanced itself from him (the company's website doesn't mention him in its history). His pallbearers were his chauffeur, his male nurse, and other personal employees.

One man was famous, courted, wealthy, connected, powerful, envied, and feared. The other man secretly scrounged for food behind a grocery store and was loved. Which one was rich toward God?

It's only stuff.

CHAPTER 9

PREVENT REGRET

What if in reality my life,
my conscious life,
has not been the right thing?
LEO TOLSTOY

We need to ask ourselves what we are doing (or not doing) with our lives now that could lead to deep regret. Life always plays in a forward direction; it never goes backward. Once a move is made, there is no going back.

I know of few more dramatic examples of regret than the life of the great Scottish essayist and historian Thomas Carlyle. He wrote eloquently about the illusions of being Master of the Board: "Many men eat finer cookery, drink dearer liquors, but in the heart of them, what increase of blessedness is there? Are they better, more beautiful, stronger, braver? Are they even what they call 'happier'? Do they look with satisfaction on more things and human faces in this God's Earth; do more things and human faces look with satisfaction on them? Not so."

To know this truth in our heads does not guarantee that we will live it. A few years before he wrote these words, Carlyle had married his secretary, Jane Welsh. She was highly intelligent and attractive, and she continued to serve as Carlyle's secretary after their marriage.

Some time after their marriage, Jane became ill. Carlyle, who was perhaps not much tempted by money, was deeply devoted to his work. He did not seem to notice his wife's ill health much. He was absorbed in what he was doing and allowed her to continue working. But she had cancer; eventually she was confined to her bed. Although Carlyle truly loved her, he found that he did not have much time to stay with her or much attention to give to her.

After several years of this, Jane died. The day of her funeral was stormy; they carried her body to the churchyard for burial through the rain and mud. Carlyle later returned to a house that was suddenly, shatteringly empty. He went upstairs to Jane's room and sat in the chair next to her bed, the chair he had had so little time for. He noticed her diary lying on the table next to her bed. He picked it up and began to read. On one entire page she had written a single line: "Yesterday he spent an hour with me and it was like heaven; I love him so."

A reality that he had somehow been too blind to see now revealed itself with crushing clarity. He had been too busy to notice how much he meant to Jane. He thought of all the times he had been preoccupied with his work and simply failed to notice her. He had not seen her suffering. He had not seen her love.

Thomas turned the page of Jane's diary. He read the words that would break his heart, that he could never forget: "I have listened all day to hear his steps in the hall, but now it is late and I guess he won't come today."

He read a little more in her book and then put it back on the table and ran out of the house. Friends finally found him back at the churchyard kneeling in the earth at the side of her grave, covered with mud. His eyes were red from weeping; tears were rolling down his face. "If only I had known, if only I had known," he cried.

After Jane's death, Carlyle made little attempt to write again. The historian lived another fifteen years but said he lived them "weary, bored, and a partial recluse."

No Living in Reverse

When my son John was very small, he loved to play with machines and gadgets by the hour. One day when he was three, he had been working with a tape recording for an hour or so. Finally, he looked up at his mom and said, "Mom, you know what the trouble with life is?"

"No, I don't. What's the trouble with life?"

Then a three-year-old boy sitting on the floor, who had thoroughly reflected on both Fisher-Price technology and the condition of human existence, made one of the most profound observations of life that I have ever heard: "The trouble with life," he said, "is that it doesn't have a rewind button."

Every day, every second, carries with it its own finality. Time is our one indisputably nonrenewable resource. "Where did the time go?" we ask when we sense we have spent the years wrongly or have taken some great gift for granted. And the answer, of course, is that it went to the same place it always has. At the end of every day, one more box in the calendar has been shifted from the future column to the past column, from possibility to history. And all of its moments can be remembered, can be celebrated or regretted, but can never be retrieved. The philosopher Simone Weil wrote, "All the tragedies that we can imagine can be reduced to just one: the passage of time." Life is one of those games in which you can only move forward.

> *Life is one of those games in which you can only move forward.*

Medical journalist Dr. Timothy Johnson writes:

Part of the pleasure of reading a novel lies in not knowing how it will turn out until we get to the last page — and then thinking back to how the characters might have lived differently had they known what the end would be like. But real life has an urgency so different from fiction; at the end, it cannot be changed! *"The meaning of life is that it stops."* We will never figure out how we should live our life unless we fully understand the significance of the fact that it will end. *And then what?*

Life does not have a rewind button, so we must seek to get it right the first time.

Commitments and Convictions

Sometime ago I read an article with a title that has stuck with me: "Do Your Commitments Match Your Convictions?" We all hold convictions about what matters most in our lives, about what we hold most dear. But when we take stock of our day-to-day actions, there is often a gap between what we value and the way we spend our time, money, or energy. So regret prevention means taking an honest look at what commitments are shaping our lives.

Binding commitments are actions or choices made in the past that tie us to a future course of action. They determine the shape of our lives. The ultimate commitment we are called to is the one God enters into with us. All our smaller choices about relationships and work and leisure are to be shaped and evaluated by how they help us keep the one great commitment. But often we drift into other commitments that keep us from living out our deepest values. The apostle Paul warned Timothy about exactly this tendency: "No one serving as a soldier gets involved in civilian affairs—he wants to please his commanding officer."

Binding commitments come in different flavors. Sometimes they are *dramatic*. For example, graduating from high school and choosing a college, getting married, and changing jobs or a career all involve highly dramatic commitments. One advantage of dramatic commitments is that they are easy to recognize. But we don't always think about their hidden costs. Sometimes people buy a home that means commuting an hour each way to work. They can see the increased square footage the purchase buys, but they don't see the cost of losing time with their family.

More often the commitments we bind ourselves to are *routine*. I may accept a task or say yes to someone's offer to serve on a committee. I may volunteer to serve at my church or take a class or shoulder some new responsibilities at work. Routine commitments may look mundane, but don't underestimate their power. Any parent who has signed up a five-year-old on a soccer team knows the time-consuming potential of the routine commitment. There are cults that place fewer demands on a person's time than soccer leagues do.

Some commitments are *unspoken*. These could include a commitment to ambition or comfort or learning. It might be playing golf or riding motorcycles or spending time in a chat room. Addictions are all a form of unspoken commitment. One of the most surprising discoveries of recovering addicts is how much *time* their addiction consumed, whether it involved sex, shopping, or substance abuse. Addictions steal hours not only to be indulged in but also to be fantasized over, funded, covered up, or regretted. They are not just habits that shame us; they rob us of our lives.

Our primary unspoken commitment, of course, is watching TV. According to time diaries, adults in America average four hours of viewing per day. Husbands and wives spend three or four times as much time watching television as they do talking to each other. It becomes habit forming and mildly addictive.

Maybe nowhere is the gap between convictions and commitments larger than in family life. Parents spend, on average, four hours a day watching TV, one hour a day shopping, and six minutes a day playing with their children.

The dramatic commitments receive most of our attention, but the routine and unspoken commitments are the ones that drive our lives. Because there are so many of them and because they come on a daily basis and individually look so small, we do not sense the gap that begins to grow between what we say matters most to us and what we are actually doing with our lives. And Jesus made the object of the game clear when he said to love the Lord your God with all your heart, soul, mind, and strength, and love your neighbor as yourself. God and people are what matter.

To help us get concrete, let's look at the four categories of regret that are the most common when people get to the end of their lives. (Remember, we are playing a game that doesn't back up for anyone.) And then we can ask where we most need to rearrange our lives to do regret prevention:

- I would have loved more deeply.
- I would have laughed more often.
- I would have given more generously.
- I would have lived more boldly.

I Would Have Loved More Deeply

Patrick Morley writes that as a young businessman he always made it a habit to ask older men their regrets. At the top of the list was: "I was so busy trying to improve my family's standard of living that, before I knew it, my children were grown and gone, and I never got to know them. Now they are too busy for me."

Some events have a built-in sense of urgency attached to them. A ringing telephone. April 15. A cholesterol level of 413. But the call to love rarely comes with urgency. Did I miss a chance to sit down on the floor with my child and play Chutes and Ladders or read a book or hear about his day at school? There will always be time for that when things settle down. Has it been awhile since I had a deep conversation with a truly good friend? I can always do it tomorrow. Is there a skill I would love to acquire, a gift I'm called to give? Would it feed my parents' hearts if I took the time to express my love for them? Does a voice inside me whisper a calling to come to know God better, or pray more deeply, or devote some time and energy to a cause greater than myself? *Someday*, I tell myself, *when my life is not so full.* And then the day is gone. "Why do they not teach you that time is a finger snap and an eye blink, and that you should not allow a moment to pass you by without taking joyous, ecstatic note of it, not wasting a single moment of its swift, breakneck current?"

> I'll do it someday, I tell myself, when my life is not so full. And then the day is gone.

You have this day. Mary Jean Irion wrote "Gift from a Hair Dryer," a mother's reflection as she combed her seven-year-old daughter's hair after a bath:

Comb and dry, comb and dry. *Soon I won't be able to do this any more*, you say to yourself, knowing that the little straight bob must inevitably yield to grown-up coiffures and ugly curlers. What will she be like at fourteen? Where will her hair be blowing then? And sixteen and eighteen — you suppose boys will love to watch her hair blow as you do now. And some of them will feel it on their faces, and one of them will marry her, and her hair will be perfect under the veil, and there will be her hair spread out on his pillow ... oh, you hate him a little and wonder where he is at this moment and whether he'll be good to her.... They will grow old together ... the gold-brown hair will be gray, and you will be gone, and then she will be gone ... this very hair that now your fingers smooth ...

All the tears of the world swim for a second in your eyes as you snatch the plug out of the socket suddenly and gather her into your arms, burying your face in the warm hairs as if you could seal this moment against all time.

But of course, you can't. Moments race by, and the years fly past — and we can't control them at all. One day the end will come, and we can't control that either. But the good news is, in light of eternity, each day that we live, each act of love, moves from potential good to realized good and will never be lost, not for all eternity.

Too often clarity only comes with age. When he was an old man, Malcolm Muggeridge wrote:

> When I look back on my life nowadays, what strikes me most forcibly about it is that what seemed at the time most significant and seductive seems now most futile and absurd. For instance, success in all of its various guises; being known and being praised; ostensible pleasures, like acquiring money or seducing women.... In retrospect, all these exercises in self-gratification seem pure fantasy, what Pascal called "licking the earth."

But you can take the love with you.

I Would Have Laughed More Often

One of my favorite scenes from the movie *City Slickers* is when a despondent Billy Crystal stands before his son's grade school class and decides to teach them a lesson they are perhaps not ready to learn.

> Value this time in your life, kids, because this is the time in your life when you still have your choices, and it goes by so quickly. When you're a teenager, you think you can do anything, and you do. Your twenties are a blur. Your thirties—you raise your family, you make a little money, and you think to yourself, *What happened to my twenties?* Your forties—you grow a little pot belly, you grow another chin. The music starts to get too loud, and one of your old girlfriends from high school becomes a grandmother.... Seventies—... you spend most of your time wandering around malls looking for the ultimate in soft yogurt and muttering, "How come the kids don't call?" ... Any questions?

If this sounds familiar, it's because it's the lesson of Ecclesiastes. A rueful Solomon stands in front of the class: "What do people get for all their hard work? Generations come and go, but nothing really changes.... No matter how much we see, we are never satisfied. No matter how much we hear, we are not content.... Everything under the sun is meaningless, like chasing the wind." Any questions?

But there is another possibility: sin, death, and guilt really have been defeated, and it's not up to us. *Gospel* really does mean "good news." The joy of the Lord really is our strength. Frederick Buechner puts it like this:

> A good joke is one that catches you by surprise—like God's, for instance. Who would have guessed that Israel of all nations would be the one God picked or Sarah would have Isaac at the age of ninety or the Messiah would turn up in a manger? Who could possibly see the duck-billed platypus coming or [the pole-sitting mystic] Simeon Stylites or the character currently occu-

pying the pulpit at First Presbyterian?... When God really gets going, even the morning stars burst into singing and all the sons of God shout for joy.

I Would Have Given More Generously

Thomas Lynch is a mortician-poet who has written a surprisingly witty book called *The Undertaking: Life Studies from the Dismal Trade*. He tells how often people instruct him about what kind of funerals they want, and his response is always the same: "The dead don't care." One of them is a wealthy, worldly Irish priest who rides in a big car and has his eye on the cardinal's job. "No bronze coffin for me," he tells Lynch at the cemetery one day. "No orchids or roses or limousines. The plain pine box is the one I want, a quiet Low Mass and the pauper's grave. No pomp and circumstance."

The priest pictures his corpse as a model of piety and simplicity. He is actually moved at the thought of having chosen such a humble and austere send-off. Lynch points out that he doesn't have to wait till he dies; he could actually give simplicity a go today. Quit the country club and do his hacking at the public links; trade in his brougham for a used Chevy; give away his Florsheims and cashmeres and prime ribs. Lynch offers to help him with this, to distribute his savings and credit cards among the worthy poor of the parish, and then, when the sad duty called, bury him for free in the manner to which he would by then have become accustomed. This suggestion is not met with enthusiasm.

"What I was trying to tell the fellow was, of course, that being a dead saint is no more worthwhile than being a dead angelfish. Living is the run, and always has been.... This is the central fact of my business—there is nothing, once you are dead, that can be done to you or with you that will do you any good or harm.... *The dead don't care*."

Ask yourself, "If I were to die, would I have any regrets about my stuff?" The time to start giving is today.

I Would Have Lived More Boldly

A friend of mine is a professional musician. For many years he made his living on the road as a performer. He was becoming increasingly successful. Then, three years ago, he became a father. He was on the road about half the time. He realized that when his daughter was about a year old, she hardly knew him. He knew he needed to make a change, but it was frightening to him. What if his career track slowed to a crawl? What if being home more actually made life harder?

He took a job as the head of a music department at a university. He still performs, but he travels now only a fraction of the time. His relationship with his daughter has become a source of pride and joy in his life that he otherwise never would have known. He did have to let go of some of his old dreams, but he has since recorded a bestselling CD and been nominated for a Grammy. Most important, he realizes his daughter will grow up a fundamentally different human being now than she would have if she had grown up with a hole in her heart where a father was supposed to be. By the end of his life, he will have a title that means much more to him than Rock Star. The title is Dad.

Don't Wait for a Crisis

One of the reasons most of us need to ask ourselves how we should rearrange our lives to prevent regret is that we suffer from "commitment creep." Creeping commitments are the crabgrass on the lawn of life. They multiply without our permission or even our awareness. Commitments are not biodegradable; they do not decompose like leaves in a forest. They stick around for eons like plastic wrappers and Styrofoam cups.

This in turn creates a condition called "active inertia." People tend to stick to old commitments, even when those commitments no longer make sense; even when they become injurious to our health or well-being or our souls. Often this goes on until we hit a crisis. And that's when we find time to change.

A busy father whose neglected daughter runs away from home and gets sucked into a life of addiction suddenly finds time to scour the country for her and then spend weeks looking for treatment clinics and rehab centers.

A couple who were too busy for each other suddenly find massive amounts of time for counseling and lawyers and legal bills and apartment searches when a marriage falls apart.

A businessperson who "had" to take ethical shortcuts and cut corners to keep up with the competition suddenly has time to reflect on right and wrong and wonder why she was living under so much pressure when she was fired for misconduct.

A workaholic, rushaholic, compulsive overachiever suddenly finds twenty-four hours a day to ask what life really means when a lab report comes back from the doctor's office marked "malignant."

One day, of course, we will face the ultimate crisis. Our earthly life will end, and we will stand before God. Jesus' story about the rich fool is a story about a man headed toward a crisis without paying attention, like a skipper admiring the beauty and soundness of his yacht about fifteen feet before plunging over Niagara Falls. If we wait long enough, the crisis will come. The crisis always comes. But it is better not to wait.

> *Creeping commitments are the crabgrass on the lawn of life. They multiply without our permission or even our awareness.*

We Have This Moment

One truth is certain: time will not slow down, and we will never be able to redo yesterday. We can't play it again, Sam.

I can remember my grandmother on road trips telling us stories from years ago in St. Francisville. She used to describe an old woman at the church where she grew up; Gram would grab the loose skin around her throat and shake it so she could sing with the warble of the old lady she was describing. And I remember wondering to myself, *Doesn't Gram know that she's an old lady?*

Fast-forward forty years. (Life does have a fast-forward button.) I'm flying to Canada, and in the seat next to me is a highly verbal four-year-old named Bobby. Bobby turns to me and addresses me: "Hey mister — you're an old guy!"

"Yes," I say to Bobby, "you're right. And if you keep talking to people like that, you're not going to have that problem."

The days go slowly, but the years go fast. Life doesn't have a rewind button.

HOW TO PLAY

CHAPTER 10

PLAY BY THE RULES

The first thing in all progress
is to leave something behind.
GEORGE MACDONALD

Every game comes with a set of rules. No spitballs. Play it where it lies. Run inside the base paths. No hitting below the belt. No sneaking money from the bank when no one's looking. No dealing from the bottom of the deck. Don't kick dust on the umpire. Always, breaking the rules means consequences. Three strikes and you're out. Roughing up the passer will cost you fifteen yards.

Sometimes people go a little overboard on the rules, particularly when they involve other people. Certain golf fans live to spot a violation on TV and call to turn in an unknowing rule breaker to tournament officials. The cricket rule book actually has a rule (part 10 of rule 42 — I'm not making this up): "10. WASTING TIME: The wasting of time shall be deemed unfair." Considering that a single cricket match can last several decades, this one seems hard to enforce. Teddy Roosevelt, for whom almost every choice carried moral implications, opposed baseball because he believed that throwing a curve ball was deceptive and therefore unethical. Manly players throw it straight.

But far more often, we find ways around rules. We cork bats, take steroids, fudge golf scores, and sneak Scrabble tiles when no one is looking. We try to hide our dishonesty, sometimes even from ourselves. Always, games test our integrity. We have words for people who achieve victory: *winners, champions.* We don't have a word for people who honor the rules. Rules bring us to the deeper issue — the issue of character. If we are clever enough, we may be able to find a way to skirt the rules, but that doesn't keep us from violating our character.

Penny Baxter found an ingenious way to lie by telling the truth. He was the hero of Marjorie Rawlings's novel *The Yearling*. He had a no-good hunting dog he wanted to unload. In the valley of the Ockla- waha River, everybody bragged about how good his hunting dog was. So when Penny Baxter began running down their dog at the village store, heads popped up. No one had ever heard a man tell the bald truth about his dog before.

Lemm Forester figured Penny must be trying to hide what a great dog he really had. He went to Penny's place the next day with a fine shotgun to make a trade. Penny protested the dog was no good; Lemm insisted: "Don't argue with me. Take the gun for him or I'll come steal him."

It worked out just as Penny had foreseen, but he felt guilty. His son tried to reassure him: "Shucks, Pa, you told the truth."

"Yes, son, my words was straight, but my intention was as crooked as the Ocklawaha River."

We can try to finesse the rules if we want to, and we may get away with it. We may even be able to convince ourselves. But we cannot finesse integrity. Aristotle said a long time ago that the central ques- tion is not just "What shall I do?" but "What kind of person shall I become?"

When I play the game, am I the kind of person other people know they can trust? And do they trust me — not because I'm clever at winning their confidence, but because I actually behave in trust- worthy ways? "Save me, O LORD, from lying lips and from deceitful tongues."

Integrity Problems Start Early and Run Deep

Some time ago, we had a moment of conflict in the car. I was quite sure one of my kids had crossed a line, but they denied it. I didn't have a smoking gun, but the circumstantial evidence was overwhelming. I was doing cross-examination, trying to get the child to break down, but this child was pretty savvy. At one point they looked up with deeply hurt, misty eyes and said with a quivering voice: "Daddy, you don't think I'd lie to you, do you?"

I started to say, "Oh, child, no, the thought never crossed my mind."

Then I stopped to think. What I said was, "Do I think you'd lie? Of course I do.

"I lie. Your mom lies, that's for sure. Everybody I've ever known has lied. The most famous story about lying in American history is the story of George Washington cutting down a cherry tree. His father asked him who did it. George is supposed to have said, 'I cannot tell a lie; it was me.' That was in a biography written by Parson Weems in the nineteenth century — he made the story up. The most famous story about not lying in America was a lie.

"Anybody who says he or she never lies is lying. Mostly I think you tell the truth, but absolutely I think you'd lie."

It got very quiet in the backseat.

Integrity issues come up all the time. Politicians spin their promises; telemarketers try to scam the elderly, white-collar workers commit a variety of crimes, job seekers pad their resumes, repair shops pad their bills, students steal essays from the Internet for school, spouses lie to each other about money or fidelity; teenagers lie to their parents about where they've been, and parents break promises they make to their children. People do these things even though they know what the Scriptures say: "Each of you must put off falsehood and speak truthfully to his neighbor." "Do not lie to each other, since you have taken off your old self with its practices." "The LORD abhors dishonest scales, but accurate weights are his delight."

Often we're so busy protesting our innocence — "You don't think I'd lie, do you?" — that we don't even notice our lack of integrity.

Often we're so busy protesting our innocence — "You don't think I'd *lie*, do you?" — that we don't even notice our lack of integrity.

When you say to someone, "Yes, I'll pray for you," do you ever not do it?

Have you ever blamed showing up late on heavy traffic or an un-avoidable delay when the truth is you just didn't allow enough time?

Ever come up with an excuse at work when the truth was you procrastinated?

Ever make a commitment and not follow through?

Ever walk off with company supplies at work, or fudge an expense account, or send in a tax return that was less than fully forthcoming? Financial expert Larry Burkett estimates that fully 50 percent of people who claim to be Christians have cheated on their taxes. The IRS maintains what is informally called a "cheaters account," to which people with guilty consciences can send money they know they owe. There's an old story that the IRS received one letter that read, "My conscience is bothering me because of cheating on taxes, so I'm sending $10,000. If my conscience doesn't clear up, I'll send in the rest of what I owe."

We want to follow the rules, but we are prepared to break them if we think we can get away with it and if that's what it takes for us to win. We are ready to cheat if that's what "doing well" at the game requires. The journey to integrity requires the cultivation of a desire: I must want to be good more than I want to do well. It requires a decision: I will choose to play with integrity and lose rather than cheat and win. It requires a belief: I cannot succeed in what I do and fail in who I am. Psychologist Martin Seligman writes:

> The belief that we can rely on shortcuts to happiness, joy, rapture, comfort, and ecstasy, rather than be entitled to these feelings by exercise of personal strengths and virtues, leads to legions of people who in the middle of great wealth are starving spiritually. Positive emotion alienated from the exercise of character leads to emptiness, to inauthenticity, to depression, and, as we age, to the gnawing realization that we are fidgeting until we die.

Integrity Is Not the Same as Knowing the Rules

Our problem generally is not that we don't know the rules, but that we don't live what we already know. A man is being tailgated by a woman who is in a hurry. He comes to an intersection, and when the light turns yellow, he hits the brakes. The woman behind him goes ballistic. She honks her horn at him; she yells her frustration in no uncertain terms; she rants and gestures.

While she is in mid-rant, someone taps on her window. She looks up and sees a policeman. He invites her out of her car and takes her to the station where she is searched and fingerprinted and put in a cell. After a couple of hours, she is released, and the arresting officer gives her her personal effects, saying, "I'm very sorry for the mistake, ma'am. I pulled up behind your car while you were blowing your horn, using bad gestures and bad language. I noticed the 'What Would Jesus Do?' bumper sticker, the 'Choose Life' license plate holder, the 'Follow Me to Sunday School' window sign, the Christian fish emblem on your trunk, and I naturally assumed you had stolen the car."

The world gets pretty tired of people who have Christian bumper stickers on their cars, Christian fish signs on their trunks, Christian books on their shelves, Christian stations on their radios, Christian jewelry around their necks, Christian videos for their kids, and Christian magazines for their coffee tables but don't actually have the life of Jesus in their bones or the love of Jesus in their hearts.

Integrity Is Not the Same as Reputation

Developing a reputation for integrity is not the same as having it. Jesus is the only person in the New Testament to use the word *hypocrite* (Greek *hypocritos*) to describe those who "do not practice what they preach." There is a picture behind this word.

Archaeologists have recently excavated a large city named Sepphoris, which was largely built by Herod when Jesus was a boy. It was visible from the hillside on which the little village of Nazareth was located. It housed a giant amphitheater, which Jesus may well have helped to construct as a young man.

The actors who put on plays there were called *hypokrites*. They wore masks so that the audience could identify the characters they were intended to play. At the end of the play, they would take off their masks and ask if the audience liked the performance enough to applaud them off the stage.

Devout Jews did not attend such spectacles because they were considered pagan. And so the word *hypokrites* does not show up elsewhere in the Scriptures. But probably as a young man, Jesus was quite familiar with this scene. And the sting it would carry for religious leaders who considered themselves devout—who would never go to such a play—was doubly painful.

I understand about *hypocrites*. I have always wrestled with this. Sometimes when I was young and at home alone watching TV, if I heard a car pull into the driveway, I would quickly turn off the TV so that when a family member came in, it would look like I was doing something productive. I say, "when I was young," but the truth is I still do that. When I was a teenager, I would pretend to my family that I was not really all that interested in girls and dating, that I was occupied by more important things. I would pretend that I was much more confident than I really was, much less worried about being rejected by a girl.

When I played in tennis tournaments, I wanted to win so badly that sometimes I would call a ball out even if it was in. I can remember a big tournament where we had an umpire who could overrule disputed calls. I called a ball out that I knew was in, and I'm sure the umpire knew it was in, but my opponent trusted me too much to dispute it.

I can remember sitting in classes taking tests and wanting so badly to get a good grade that I would look on the paper of the person next to me to see what answer he or she gave. Once in a math class a teacher caught me and kept me after class to talk about it. I responded in a way that even now seems odd to me: I pointed out that even if I had gotten that particular question wrong, my test score would have remained the same. To this he replied, of course, that that was not the point, that he thought I would be more concerned about the fact that I had cheated. And I was mortified when he said this. But I'm not sure even now if I was more pained by what I had done or by the fact that I had gotten caught. I think that how people saw me mattered more to me than who I actually was on the inside. I think I preferred to cheat secretly and get the perks that go with being thought smarter than I am than to be honest but risk having grades a little lower. To this day, I cannot talk about these events without feeling pain inside at what they say about my character. Hypocrisy, someone said, is the homage vice pays to virtue. It is also the pain that actors feel when the applause dies away.

> In a strict sense, I cannot break the rules. They endure, for they reflect the way things are. I can only break myself against them.

We break rules—we violate God's will—because we think breaking them will help us win, or at least avoid pain. But what we do not see is that the very breaking of them turns us into the kind of people who are increasingly incapable of the gratitude and purity of heart that makes lasting happiness and meaning possible. In a strict sense, I cannot break the *rules*. They endure, for they reflect the way things are. I can only break myself against them.

"Sin-Avoidance" Is Not the Same as Integrity

The greatest talk ever given on what goodness looks like was delivered by Jesus in what is called the Sermon on the Mount. He starts with a section called beatitudes: "Blessed are the poor in spirit, for theirs is the kingdom of heaven. Blessed are those who mourn, for they will be comforted," and so on. People love that. People print those words on plaques and hang them in their homes.

Then Jesus described redeemed humanity: "You are the salt of the earth. . . . You are the light of the world." People love that. They print those words on plaques and hang them in their homes.

Then he spoke of anger and lust in the human heart, and advised: "If your right eye causes you to sin, gouge it out and throw it away. . . . And if your right hand causes you to sin, cut it off and throw it away. It is better for you to lose one part of your body than for your whole body to go into hell." You hardly ever see that one hanging on a wall. It seems a little cranky. It's worth thinking about what Jesus is up to here. Is Jesus actually proposing dismemberment as a spiritual growth strategy?

Sometimes churches have membership ceremonies as part of their services. Should they have "dismembership" ceremonies as well? "I've been gossiping a little too much—next week my tongue's coming out."

I don't think so. I think Jesus is engaged in a fundamental discussion about what makes someone good in God's eyes. People often define goodness in terms of sin avoidance. For the scribes and Pharisees, this meant don't disobey the Torah. Don't break the rules.

So if integrity means avoiding adultery, I could simply seek to avoid all women. And in Jesus' day this was the strategy of a group known as the 'blind and bleeding rabbis,' because not only would they never speak to a woman, but they would close their eyes when one came into their peripheral vision and so were forever falling off curbs and bumping into buildings.

On the behavior modification plan, I define integrity as "sin avoidance." As long as I'm not engaged in forbidden behaviors, I think I'm on the right track. So Jesus says, "If God's goal for you is sin avoidance, here's a good idea: whack off any part of your body that might do something wrong, and you'll roll right into heaven a mutilated stump."

This approach reminds me of a scene in a movie called *Monty Python and the Holy Grail*. King Arthur is accosted by the Black Knight who has murder in his heart. They fight, and one-by-one the Black Knight loses both arms and legs. He still yells for Arthur to come back and fight. "What are you going to do—bleed on me?" asks Arthur. The Black Knight is a mutilated stump. He will not violate the commandment "Thou shall not kill." But there is murder in his heart. He would kill — if he could.

My eye, hand, and foot are not the problem. The problem is my heart. Integrity is much bigger than simply avoiding breaking the rules. It is becoming the kind of person who does the right thing. Integrity does not mean I get really good at not doing the things I really want to do. It is not using lots of willpower to override my desires. It means I become the kind of person who actually wants to do what is right.

Thinking I'm Okay Doesn't Guarantee Integrity

My problem is not just my lack of character; it is that I can't even see how badly I lack it. Humans have an almost limitless capacity for self-deception. For instance, psychologists speak of a massive integrity blind spot in human nature called the self-serving bias. We make ourselves the heroes of our stories to exaggerate our role in victories and to absolve ourselves of blame for failure and error.

In one survey, 800,000 high school students were asked whether they were above or below average in social skills. If they were accurate, they should have split 50 – 50. Want to guess what percentage of students rated themselves as below average? Zero percent! Furthermore, 25 percent of all students rated themselves in the top 1 percent!

This self-serving bias extends to every area. The majority of people in hospitals suffering from crashes that they themselves caused rate themselves as above-average

> *My problem is not just my lack of character; it is that I can't even see how badly I lack it.*

drivers! You might think that education would make us more self-aware. You'd be wrong: 88 percent of college professors rated themselves above average; 25 percent rated themselves as truly exceptional. Another survey of two hundred sociologists found that half believed they would become one of the top ten sociologists in the world. No wonder there are such conflicts around tenure and promotion.

National surveys show that we claim to feel nine years younger than we actually are, and we claim that we look five years younger than other people our age.

And the church is not exempt. George Barna did a survey of pastors — people who are paid to teach on texts like Paul's command to the church at Rome: "Do not think of yourself more highly than you ought, but rather think of yourself with sober judgment." Ninety percent of us consider ourselves above-average preachers.

And perhaps most ironic of all: when people have the concept of the self-serving bias carefully explained to them, the majority of people rate themselves as well above average in their ability to handle the self-serving bias!

Another integrity problem we have is called the "fundamental attribution error." It works like this: If something good happens in my life, I tend to explain it by taking credit for it; but if I fail, I tend to explain by blaming circumstances. If I do well on a test, I think it's because I'm smart; if I do poorly, it's because I was distracted. If people like my message, it's because I'm a good preacher; if they don't like it, it's because they are obstinate or have the attention span of a fruit fly.

What makes the fundamental attribution error even worse is the way we explain the behavior of other people. We tend to explain our bad behavior in terms of mitigating circumstances; we tend to explain other people's bad behavior in terms of their character defects. If *I* yell at *my* child in the grocery store, it's because they have misbehaved to an extent that would exhaust the patience of Job. If *you* yell at *your* child in the grocery store, it's obvious that you're an anger management problem waiting to happen who never should have been granted a parenting license in the first place. If *I* get a speeding ticket, it's because the police needed to fill their quota, so they set up a trap when they should have been out catching criminals. If *you* get a speeding ticket, it shows what a careless driver you are.

If you want still more evidence of our capacity for self-deception, read the survey done by *U.S. News and World Report* in 1997, which asked people, "Who do you think is most likely to get into heaven?"

Mother Teresa	79%	(apparently 21% of the respondents grade pretty high!)
Oprah	66%	
Michael Jordan	65%	
Colin Powell	61%	
Dennis Rodman	28%	
O.J. Simpson	19%	

One vote getter topped even Mother Teresa. One individual got an 87 percent shot at getting past the pearly gates. Want to guess who? It was the person completing the survey. Apparently people's thoughts ran like this: *Out of all the famous people in the world, I'd put Mother Teresa at the top, but there's one person I'd have to say has a better shot than Mother Teresa* — me!

When We Break the Rules

The way back home for rule breakers is the way of grace through repentance. We need God's help to see the truth about our lives and character. Often he will enlighten us not only through times of reflection but through other people who see and know us well. And then we need to reroute our lives.

Recently I spoke at the college my daughter Laura attends. We had lunch together, then I drove to the airport to fly home. Nancy and I were going to be home alone that night, and we had a special evening planned, so I was looking forward to it. On the way to the airport, I was on a road curving around the rim of a foothill in Santa Barbara, and I came to an intersection where Laura had said I needed to turn left to get to the airport. But that was a narrow little road. I was on a big broad road curving around the mountain and could see the Pacific Ocean in all its immense beauty. So I said

> *The way back home for rule breakers is the way of grace through repentance.*

to myself: "I'll take the broad way. If I go on that narrow road, I'll lose all this beauty. I want to take the scenic route. There is a way that seemeth right to me."

So on I went. The broad road kept curving and twisting, not getting me where I needed to go. The clock was ticking; I could miss my flight. A little voice inside me said, *Turn around. Go back the other way. Take the narrow road.*

I said, "I'd feel like an idiot."

The little voice said, *You are an idiot.*

I knew better. But I would not turn around. Sheer pride. Stubbornness.

The clock was ticking.

I got to the airport. I was racing by now. The ticket agent said to me: "Sorry. The gate has been shut. The doors are locked. The plane's leaving. You've been left behind."

There was weeping, wailing, and gnashing of teeth. No matter how hard I gnashed them, that plane was not coming back.

The good news is that true repentance never leads to despair. It leads home. It leads to grace. Jack Nicholson delivers a great line to Helen Hunt in the film *As Good as It Gets*: "You make me want to be a better man." When people do that for us, they become vessels of grace.

Better than all else is living with the Grace Giver, the only one who ever fully understood and lived the rules. In the words of the great Scottish preacher James Stalker, "The most important part of the training of the Twelve was one which was perhaps at the time little noticed, though it was producing splendid results—the silent and constant influence of his character on them. It was this which made them into the men they became."

CHAPTER 11

FILL EACH SQUARE WITH WHAT MATTERS MOST

Those who rush
arrive first at the grave.
SPANISH PROVERB

The board that you and I play on comes in the shape of a calendar. It is filled with squares, and each square is another day. We live one square at a time. A very wise Dutchman by the name of Lewis Smedes wrote about this several decades ago.

> I bought a brand-new date book yesterday, the kind I use every year—spiral-bound, black imitation leather covers wrapped around pages and pages of blank boxes. Every square has a number to tell me which day of the month I'm in at the moment. Every square is a frame for one episode of my life. Before I'm through with the book, I will fill the squares with classes I teach, people with whom I ate lunch, everlasting committee meetings I sit through, and these are only the things I cannot afford to forget. I fill the squares too with things I do not write down to remember: thousands of cups of coffee, some lovemaking, some praying, and, I hope, gestures of help to my neighbors. Whatever I do, it has to fit inside one of those squares on my date book. I live one square at a time. The four lines that make up the box are the walls of time that organize my life. Each box has an invisible door that leads to the next square. As if by a silent stroke, the door

opens and I am pulled through, as if by a magnet, sucked into the next square in line. There I will again fill the time frame that seals me—fill it with my busy-ness just as I did the square before. As I get older, the squares seem to get smaller. One day I will walk into a square that has no door. There will be no mysterious opening and no walking into an adjoining square. One of those squares will be terminal. I do not know which square it will be.

We are all square fillers. Most of us have a sense that our squares are too chaotic, stuffed with too much activity, but that we'll get around to what matters most one day *when things settle down.*

I was part of a survey that asked thousands of people what kept them from knowing and loving God better. The number one answer was "I'm too busy." It's ironic that the early followers of Jesus could not be stopped by persecution, poverty, prison, or martyrdom. But we're stunted by something as trivial as too much to do.

I sometimes do a talk using props to illustrate what Smedes was talking about: an empty glass jar, a pitcher full of sand, and four tennis balls. The idea is not original with me, and I'm not sure where it started. The empty glass jar, about the size of a half-gallon milk carton, represents your life. It is a finite thing. There are limitations to it. But one way or another, it's going to get filled up. The tennis balls are marked with the letters G, P, C, and J. We will come back to them later.

The Have-tos

The sand in the pitcher represents the "have-tos" of your life, all the things you are obliged to do. We will review some of them together. For every item, picture a little more sand being poured into the jar that is your life.

First, you have some work have-tos. You have things to get done at an office or school or home. You have a boss to manage, meetings to attend, projects to complete. You have to manage chaos. Dr. Richard

Swenson writes that the average desk worker in our society has thirty-six hours worth of work piled up on his or her desk and spends three hours a week just sorting through all the piles looking for stuff. You will spend fifty-two minutes a day on the phone and another fifteen minutes a day on hold. The hours we devote to work keep increasing, despite Benjamin Franklin's prediction that because of technological advances, we would be working four hours a week. Each of the above tasks is represented by a little more sand being poured into the jar of your life.

Then you have personal tasks to take care of. You have to sleep — that's six to eight hours a night. You have to take a shower, brush your teeth, floss your teeth (for at least a week or so after you visit the dentist and the hygienist is repulsed by how filthy your teeth are). You have to exercise occasionally, and if you don't go to the doctor once in a while, you will pay for it in the long run. More sand in the jar.

You also have household jobs to do. Someone has to buy food, prepare food, and clean up. And, of course, we all have to take time to eat. We buy microwave ovens to save time, but research shows that they only save four minutes a day. "We are a nation that shouts at a microwave oven to hurry up," writes accountant Joan Ryan. Comedian Steve Wright jests, "I put my instant coffee in my microwave oven and almost went back in time." Somebody has to wash the clothes and mow the grass. Furnaces must be maintained and gutters cleaned. Bills have to get paid. Checkbooks have to get balanced. You can save a little time by starting a second checking account and waiting until the first account clears and letting the bank figure out how much you have.

When Nancy and I got married, I asked her which household task she most disliked. Her response was immediate: cleaning the bathroom. "Well, I want to take that chore off your plate," I said. "You will never have to worry about that one." And she hasn't. In over twenty years of marriage, she's never cleaned the bathroom. I haven't either. They're a mess. But at least it saves time.

The technology that is supposed to save us time becomes part of our burden. Juliet Shor notes in *The Overworked American* that when automatic washers and driers were introduced, the amount of time people spent doing laundry actually *increased* because our standards for what counts as "clean" kept rising.

> The technology that is supposed to save us time becomes part of our burden.

You will spend time on the technology that is supposed to save you time. My dental hygienist recently gave me an electric toothbrush so I could brush my teeth more efficiently; it came with a thirty-one-page instruction manual that said I was supposed to read it *carefully* before using the toothbrush.

When VCRs hit the market, they became wildly successful, in part because they promised control over time: people could finally record whatever they wanted and watch it whenever they desired. The only problem was that it took so long to comprehend the instructions, that people who bought the VCRs would die before they could figure them out. And when they died and the paramedics carried off their cold, lifeless bodies, the paramedics would list the time of death as 12:00 because that was the time blinking on the VCR.

Other Obligations

We all have to take time to maintain relationships as well. We have social obligations. If you have children, you have school, music lessons, sports leagues, and sleepovers to take them to. You have relatives. Sand, sand, sand.

You will, if you're average, spend thirty-one minutes a day on child care. You will also spend seven minutes a day on plant and/or pet care, and sixteen minutes a day (roughly one year of your life) looking for lost objects. You will spend twenty-nine minutes a day visiting other people—a figure that has declined dramatically over the decades. And you will spend four minutes a day filling out paperwork for the government. Sand, sand, sand. Your little jar is filling up.

Then there is car time. You will spend six months of your life at traffic lights. If you're average, you spend seventy-five minutes a day commuting. To save time, you multitask. The second and third most dangerous tasks people engage in while driving are talking on cell phones and applying makeup (you know who you are). The most dangerous activity is reading. (If you are driving at the moment, please stop reading.)

Then there's recreation, because we have to do something to unwind: movies, television, newspapers, hobbies, vacations. Add to that the unexpected. Things happen that we do not plan, complicating further our already full lives. Someone gets sick, the car breaks down, Aunt Edna comes to visit, an emergency happens at work, a child misses the school bus. We'd like to believe we can eliminate the unexpected. One medical ad targeted "women who don't have time for a yeast infection" as opposed to all the slackers out there who have plenty of room in their schedules for one. More sand.

Years ago I read a newspaper article in which the writer asked experts in a variety of fields (sleep researcher, vocational coach, financial planner, physical trainer, family therapist, and so on) how much time people needed to devote per day in their particular area just to get by — not excel, just do the minimum. Added together, the "minimum requirements" for life management totaled up to thirty-six hours a day.

By this time, the little grains of sand have pretty much filled up the jar that is my life. Juggling the have-tos is challenging enough, but there are other things I want in my life, things that matter more.

Jesus said, "Seek first the kingdom of God and His righteousness, and all these things shall be added to you." This brings us to the four tennis balls. They represent activities I must engage in to pursue life in God's kingdom. Since the jar is my one and only life, I must try to squeeze the tennis balls in there somehow.

G

The first tennis ball has the initial G on it, which stands for *God*. Of course, God is not one priority among many; he is *the priority*. But there are certain things I need to do to help me remember him. I don't want to "skim" God. I don't want to get to the end of my life and not know God. I don't want every prayer I ever pray to be "Help!"

I would like to grow before I leave this planet. I have some sins and habits in my life that I'd like to make some headway on. I have a kind of legacy I want to leave for my children. I have other patterns I don't want to pass on, and I'd like to make headway on them.

I'd like to immerse my mind in Scripture. I think it is the most amazing Book the human race has ever received. I think of Psalm 1, which describes a man who is like a tree planted by waters that give life, whose life is marked by flourishing, whose delight is in the law of the Lord. This is how God says our lives should be lived. I'd like to have a life like that.

And I know this means I will have to make time to withdraw from human contact and noise and the busyness of life and make space to be alone with God. I know Jesus arranged his life on a regular basis around solitude with God. "Very early in the morning, while it was still dark, Jesus ... went off to a solitary place, where he prayed."

> *Spending an entire day alone with God may sound scary or difficult to pull off. But think of not doing it.*

I remember the first time I decided I would try to devote a whole day to solitude. I said to myself, "The next free day that comes along I will spend alone with God."

Know how long I waited? A free day never came along. I had to write it down on my calendar ahead of time. And I have had to do that ever since.

Spending an entire day alone with God may sound scary or difficult to pull off. But think of *not* doing it. Imagine reaching the age of seventy, having received more than 25,000 days as a gift from God, and not having given a single one back to him because you were "too busy."

P

The second tennis ball is marked with a *P*, and that stands for *people*. I want to be deeply present with the people in my life. I want to notice and treasure my wife and Laura and Mallory and Johnny. I want to grow some deep friendships. I'd like to be a good neighbor. I want to savor the people I work with. I'd like some folks to miss me when I'm gone. I don't want them to remember a briefcase and a closed door and a list of things to do.

One of the striking aspects of Jesus' life is the way he could pay attention to whomever he was with. He had many demands on his life, but he was never distracted or preoccupied. When someone asked him a question, he never replied, "Huh? I wasn't listening."

People take time. Relationships cannot be microwaved. Intimacy is never convenient.

Years ago Nancy and I took our three then preschoolers to Kinderphoto to get a family picture. I don't know who invented Kinderphoto, but whoever did should be put away for a long time. All three children were terrified of the experience and did not like the strange man behind the camera. All were crying and upset.

I went through a series of stages. The first was naïve optimism. "Come on kids, this will be fun." That was a short stage.

The second was bribery. "There's a Mrs. Field's cookie shop in the mall. If you will smile nicely, we will take you there for cookies." That didn't last much longer.

Bribery gave way to the threat stage. "You kids want to cry—I'll show you something to cry about." This is not a good smile inducer for preschoolers. By this time, children in other people's families were crying in the waiting room just looking at my family. I was getting embarrassed. I pulled Mallory aside because she was the most upset of our three children.

"Mallory, you're pretty sad, huh?" Big tears. Big nod.

"Mallory, I bet I know what you want right now. I bet more than anything else, you'd like to have Baby Tweezers."

Baby Tweezers was Mallory's first and most favorite doll. Mallory named her all by herself. Baby Tweezers. We're not sure why. Mallory was not a forceps delivery child. But she nodded again — that's what she wanted.

"Well, Mallory," I said, "if you ever want to see Baby Tweezers alive again ..."

In that moment, I was not at all concerned for the eternal well-being of three immortal souls. I just wanted behavioral compliance. I did not want to take the time or effort that would be required to understand my children's fears. I was irritated and in a hurry.

When the jar that is my life gets too full of have-tos, I find myself with little time for people. This is not what I want. I know that every human life is a miracle. I want to notice people who are hurting. I want to notice the poor. I want to serve and learn from people of different cultures and persons of different color. I want a compassionate heart. But that cannot happen if the box of my life is already filled with too many have-tos.

C

My third tennis ball carries the letter C for *calling*. I would like the world to be a little different because I was in it for a while. I would like to add a little value. Like the Blues Brothers, I would like to have a mission from God.

A Thousand Clowns is a play about an eccentric character raising his thirteen-year-old nephew. At one point the social services people are thinking about taking the boy away, and his uncle explains why he isn't finished with the boy yet:

> I want to be sure he knows when he's chickening out on himself. I want him to get to know exactly the special thing he is or he won't notice it when it starts to go. I want a little guts to show before I can let him go. I want to be sure he sees all the wild possibilities. I want him to know it's worth all the trouble just to give

the world a little goosing when you get the chance. And I want him to know the sneaky, subtle, important reason why he was born a human being and not a chair.

I want to know more about that sneaky, subtle, important reason God made me the way he did. I want to be honest about my gifts and limitations. I want to use what I have been given to do God's work in the world. Paul wrote to Timothy: "Devote yourself to the public reading of Scripture, to preaching and to teaching. *Do not neglect your gift.*" I want to develop whatever gifts God has given me, but gift development almost never happens for me if I let my schedule drift.

I also know that when I simply drift, my "calling" quickly turns into self-serving. Some time ago, Nancy and I were on a plane and I was reading a book called *Heroism and the Christian Life* in preparation for a talk I was to give. A small girl, probably two years old, was sitting behind me kicking her legs rhythmically into my seat. I started to get irritated. She was one of three small children traveling with their parents. Her six-month-old brother was screaming. I wanted to ask the flight attendant if they could play outside.

Then the thought occurred to me: *I'm reading a book on Christian heroism, about missionaries and martyrs, and I'm bitter because of a two-year-old.* I turned to the mom. "You know, it wasn't all that long ago that my wife and I had three children your kids' ages. I remember how hard that was. If there's anything my wife can do for you on this flight …" It will take some time for me to live on mission.

J

The fourth tennis ball is marked with the letter J, and that stands for *joy.* Jesus gave a kind of mission statement for his teaching one time: "I have told you this so that my joy may be in you and that your joy may be complete." Based on this statement alone, we can conclude that Jesus had a well-recognized capacity for joy that drew people to him. And his plan for his followers was that they be joy sharers. Paul made it a command: "Rejoice in the Lord always. I will say it again: Rejoice!"

One of the primary barriers that prevents people from wanting to know God is joy-impaired Christians. There was a rabbinic tradition in Jesus' day that a devout Jew would bless God at least one hundred times a day. It would start with waking up: "Blessed art Thou, O Sovereign of the Universe, that you have delivered me from darkness and opened my eyes."

I would like to get up to one hundred blessings a day. I want to celebrate sunsets. I want to celebrate the smell of freshly mown grass. I want to celebrate banana cream pie. I want to celebrate God's goodness and his amazing, wonderful, mysterious, holy gift of life. Physician Bernie Siegel wrote, "I've done the research and I hate to tell you, but everybody dies — lovers, joggers, vegetarians and non-smokers. I'm telling you this so that some of you who jog at 5 a.m. and eat vegetables will occasionally sleep late and have an ice cream cone."

> One of the primary barriers that prevents people from wanting to know God is joy-impaired Christians.

Regret for What We Did Not Do

By now the jar that is my life is filled with have-tos. There is no room for the tennis balls. In life as usual, there is no space for what we say matters most.

This problem, which seems so trivial, so logistical, is perhaps the greatest spiritual challenge we face. My guess is that if you are reading this book, you are not living in a consistent attitude of defiance toward God. I think the greater danger is, as Paul put it, that the world will "squeeze you into its own mold." The danger is that you will lead a respectable, decent, nonscandalous, busy, tired, human-powered life. That is unspeakably sad. We all want to pursue the kingdom of God. We just don't have the time.

What the famous columnist Sydney Harris wrote is true: "Regret for the things we did can be tempered by time; it is regret for the things we did not do that is inconsolable." Many people tell themselves: "I'll get around to these priorities when I have more time. My current condition of busyness is an aberration. I just need more hours in a day."

God, however, has ordained the numbers of hours every jar should contain. The jar only comes in size 24. It cannot be supersized. Jesus said, "Who of you by worrying [or running fast or being busy or drinking more coffee] can add a single hour to his life?" The jar isn't getting any bigger. And the tennis balls are not fitting in.

Waiting, Squeezing, Microwaving

Some people wait for their lives to get less demanding. They're usually in for a long wait. Jesus made a forecast in Matthew 6:34: "Do not worry about tomorrow, for tomorrow will worry about itself. Each day has enough trouble of its own." What's Jesus' forecast? Trouble today, trouble tomorrow. We live in a fallen world. If you wait for days to get easier before you get around to what matters, you may wait a long time.

Some people think they can squeeze everything into the box if they just try hard enough. They don't want to pay the price of *not* doing anything, so they just keep trying to jam more into their schedules. Sooner or later they end up with all the peace and serenity of a disgruntled postal employee.

Sometimes people try another approach. They attempt to microwave their priorities into marble-size commitments so they can squeeze them in alongside everything else. Pray on the run, skim over relationships, serve when they can, look for occasional laughs at a movie or a party. Many people aren't really living their priorities. They're just trying to do guilt management.

An old saying goes, "If the devil cannot make you bad, he will make you busy." Either way you miss out on the life God intended for you to lead.

The early church did not explode the way it did because people figured out how to reduce worship, prayer, serving, and community to marble-size mini-commitments that fit in around life as usual. Life as usual had to go. And it had to be replaced with something better. In fact, Jesus' early followers were called "people of the Way" because they followed the way of life Jesus had established. One of the great illusions of our day is that we can have Jesus' life without following Jesus' way. We sometimes live as if what Jesus said was "Seek ye first all these other things, and the kingdom of God shall be added unto you."

So, here's the radical idea: take the jar that is your life, and empty out all the sand. Start your day with an empty jar. Begin by devoting your time to honoring your deepest commitments. Trust God with your time. Trust that if God wants the lawn to get mowed and the snow to get shoveled, he will help you find a way to get it done. Maybe some things won't get done. Comedian-actress Roseanne Barr once said, "I feel that if the kids are still alive when my husband gets home from work, then, hey, I've done my job. When Sears comes out with a riding vacuum cleaner, then I'll clean the house." English actor-writer Quentin Crisp advised, "There is no need to do any housework at all. After the first four years the dirt doesn't get any worse. It's simply a question of not losing your nerve."

> Here's the radical idea: take the jar that is your life, and empty out all the sand. Start your day with an empty jar.

God never gives anyone too much to do.

At this point in the demonstration, I take all the sand out of the jar and put the tennis balls in first. Then I pour all the sand back in, and it fills in the empty spaces. The audience always applauds at this point. I don't know why. Maybe because it looks like magic. But it's really just making sure you start with what matters most. This doesn't mean that if I honor priorities I can do everything *I* want. But it does mean that God gives me enough time to do what God wants me to do. God never calls us to do something and fails to give us enough time to do it.

If you have any doubt about this, take a look at the tenth chapter of Joshua. Israel was engaged in a battle, but they were running out of time. Joshua cried out to God, and God responded by causing the sun to stop in the middle of the sky and delay going down about a full day. There had never been a day like it. Moreover, just as God multiplied five loaves and two fish because he's Lord over stuff, he can multiply minutes and hours because he's Lord over time. Unlike your boss, God has never given anyone too much to do. If we find ourselves in that position, it is not God's fault.

"Every square is a frame for one episode of my life," Lewis Smedes wrote. Nobody knows how many squares he or she will get, but each of us must choose how we will fill them. *You* must choose — not your boss, not your corporation, not your parents, not your friends, not your spouse, not your kids, not your peers. It is tempting to think that our jobs make us too busy or that our families place too many demands on us or that the years go by too fast. But they go at the same rate they always have. Time is ruthlessly egalitarian. Pawns and kings alike have exactly the same number of seconds in every day. God has given each of us a day with the same amount of time, and it is enough time to do what God wants us to do.

The Final Square

"We live one square at a time," said Smedes. "As we get older, they seem to get smaller. One of the squares will be terminal. But we do not know which square it will be."

A few years ago, when he was eighty-one years old, Smedes was up on a ladder putting Christmas lights around the outside of his house. He slipped and fell and hit his head and went into a coma and died a few days later. That final box, the one he had written about decades ago, came one day for him.

Smedes's life looked nothing like what he thought it would starting out. He came from a family of blacksmiths, but he didn't get the right body. When he graduated from high school, he was six feet four inches tall and weighed 120 pounds. He tried to sign up for the army when World War II broke out, but the doctor just laughed and told him the country needed soldiers but not that badly. On the way home, Smedes stopped by the Red Cross to donate blood; when he took off his shirt, they told him he needed his blood more than they did. He would never make it as a soldier or a blacksmith, so he filled his boxes with teaching and writing and friendship that touched thousands of lives.

There are, Smedes wrote, only two options about the final square. One is that it turns out to be a coffin. "I may have strutted my petty pace through all these squares pretending to be somebody special; now I may share my bed with the rats." That is, it may be that when we die, we go out like so many candles in the wind and that one day, a million or a billion years from now, everything will be dark.

The second possibility is that when we walk into that final square, it isn't a box at all; it turns out to be a door. The four walls that have confined us melt away, and time is no more. And our real life, far from being over, turns out to have just begun.

The Christian gospel comes down to a promise from Jesus that the last option is the real one. The last square is an opening into a new world where God will set everything right. One day you will enter it, and so will I.

In the meantime, fill your squares wisely.

CHAPTER 12

ROLL
THE DICE

Boredom ought to be one
of the seven deadly sins.

FREDERICK BUECHNER

Here is the irrefutable truth about games that my grandmother would try to teach me as she risked everything for Boardwalk while I tried to hang on to my little cache: when you start the game, you never know what the outcome will be. If you play the game, you may lose. But if you never play the game, you definitely will never win.

And if you play the game, you have to roll the dice.

What do you think is the most dangerous object in your home?

Larry Lauden is a University of Hawaii philosophy professor who has written a book about risk in which he devotes an entire chapter to household dangers. Some are what you'd expect: 460,000 people a year are injured by kitchen knives; manual and power saws account for about 100,000 injuries a year. But some risks are surprising. Got any draperies? Every year 20 people in America are strangled to death by drapery cords. Some 4,000 of us seriously injure ourselves on pillows.

But I think the most dangerous object in your home is one that not even Larry Lauden talks about. It's a back-reclining, deeply cushioned, foot-resting little death trap called an easy chair (usually spelled EZ because using only two letters takes less effort). We don't buy these chairs because of their beauty. And they are not called "challenge chairs" or "adventure chairs." They're EZ, and we buy them for one reason: comfort.

I want to give you a picture of what this chair can do. So imagine donning your sweats, putting on slippers, and breaking out your favorite kind of food—comfort food—Oreos and a cold glass of milk.

What's the single most important device someone sitting in this chair needs to hold in his hand? A remote control. I was at a friend's house recently and discovered that TV manufacturers have actually invented a remote for children called a "Wee-mote" (I'm not making this up) so the little addicts can get a head start on learning how to handle the remote.

Imagine sprawling out in that chair with the lights turned low, comfort food on a tray at your side, the remote in your hand, and the world locked outside your door. Do you feel ready to spring into action? Are you poised for an explosion of growth and development? If God asks you to do a difficult thing, are you likely to say yes?

If this is what your life is about—pursuing comfort and trying to minimize problems and stress and maximize safety and security—does this idea make your heart beat faster? Would you be excited about getting out of bed every morning to head for this chair? Do you think you will even be able to stay awake for the rest of this chapter?

That little amoeba had no stress, no problems, no challenges. Know what happened to it? It died. Too much comfort is lethal.

What's so dangerous about this chair is not the things you do while you're in it. It's the things you don't do, the relationships you never deepen, the people in need you never serve—never even see. It's the great prayers you never pray, noble thoughts you never think, adventures you never take. It's the races you never run and the battles you never fight, the laughs you don't laugh and the tears you don't weep. You were made for something more than life in the chair. It may be the most dangerous object in your house.

Scientists at Berkeley did a study years ago. They put an amoeba in an ideal environment: perfect temperature, perfect humidity, perfect amount of light, perfect food conditions. That little amoeba had no stress, no problems, no challenges. Know what happened to it? It died. Too much comfort is lethal.

A Man Can't Just Sit There

Larry Walker always wanted to fly, but poor eyesight disqualified him from pilot status in the air force. So he got an idea.

He hitched up forty-five helium-filled weather balloons to his lawn chair, strapped himself in with some sandwiches, a pellet gun, and a six-pack of lite beer. (That tells us a fair amount about Larry right there.) His plan was to hover 30 feet or so above the backyard for a few hours, then shoot enough balloons to come down.

But forty-five weather balloons holding thirty-three cubic feet of helium apiece do not settle for 30 feet. When his friends cut the cord anchoring his lawn chair to the ground, Larry did not level off at 100 feet. Nor 1,000. He stopped climbing at 16,000 feet (only in Los Angeles!).

At this height he was reluctant to shoot anything. He drifted with his beer and sandwiches into the airspace of LAX. (I told this story at a gathering once that included a Delta pilot who had been flying that day. He told me that every radio communiqué reporting this man to the tower began with the same words: "You're not going to believe this, but ...")

After several hours, Larry decided to risk shooting a few balloons and eventually descended enough to get tangled up in some power lines, where he was rescued. The FAA spokesman said, "We know he broke some part of the Federal Aviation Act, and as soon as we figure out which part it was, a charge will be filed." As they led Larry away in handcuffs, a reporter asked him why he did it.

Larry replied: "A man can't just sit there."

Larry may not score real high on the discretion scale. His story merited inclusion in *The Darwin Awards*, a book about people who through incredibly stupid acts elevate the IQ of the human race by eliminating themselves from the gene pool. Larry only got an honorable mention because he actually survived. But he's right about one thing. A man can't just sit there.

We must have challenge, risk, adventure.

God Specializes in Problem Distribution

When I say life is too short to play it safe all the time, I'm not talking about doing something impulsive or stupid. This is not about going over Niagara Falls in a barrel or betting your life's savings on the Cubs. It's really about making life an adventuresome partnership with God.

We find in the Bible numerous "call narratives," or accounts of God "calling" ordinary people to do specific assignments. God's call comes before we roll the dice. Scholars have identified a consistent pattern to these stories. Let's walk through some of them together and see what they mean for us.

1. Initial Call

God summons someone to serve him. You may have noticed that very rarely in the Bible does God bother to interrupt someone's life and ask him or her to do an easy task. He doesn't call Moses over to a burning bush and ask him if he could take on a few more sheep. One entire chapter in the Bible, Hebrews 11, is devoted to a series of encounters where God asks people to embrace high-risk assignments. God asks Noah to build an ark in the face of ridicule, Abraham to leave everything familiar and then to become a father at the age of ninety-nine, Joseph to be faithful in the face of slavery and imprisonment, and Moses to defy Pharaoh.

Listen to how the writer of Hebrews describes people who say yes to God:

> I do not have time to tell about ... [those] who through faith conquered kingdoms, administered justice, and gained what was promised; who shut the mouths of lions, quenched the fury of

the flames, and escaped the edge of the sword; whose weakness was turned to strength; and who became powerful in battle and routed foreign armies.... Others were tortured and refused to be released.... Some faced jeers and flogging, while still others were chained and put in prison. They were stoned; they were sawed in two; they were put to death by the sword.... the world was not worthy of them.

How high a value would you say God places on making sure people who follow him lead comfortable lives? It seems that God wants to use us, wants to grow us up, wants us to be strong and wise and courageous. He doesn't appear to be terribly interested in making sure we're comfortable. He would not make a good flight attendant.

2. Response

In these call narratives, in every case the person God interrupts gives his or her initial reaction directly to God. If you are at all familiar with the Bible, ask yourself whether you have heard the following responses from those to whom God has given hard assignments: What a great opportunity! Defy Pharaoh. Take on the Midianites. Spend a night in the lions' den. Walk into the fiery furnace. Marry a pregnant girl who claims she's still a virgin. Face jeers, flogging, chains, prison. Fabulous! What a great challenge — can we supersize it?

Almost always the response is fear. I mention this because sometimes people say things like, "God would never ask me to do something that I'm scared to do," or "God would never ask me to do something that I can't handle." One of the most misquoted passages in the Bible is from Paul's letter to the church at Corinth. Paul says, "[God] will not let you be tempted beyond what you can bear." Paul's point is that we can never worm out of responsibility for sin by saying it's God's fault. People twist that statement into saying that God will never give us more than we can handle. Really? Look around the world: holocaust, death, martyrdom, cancer, war. Whether it's a special assignment or just living in a fallen world, people all the time are given burdens they cannot handle.

When God calls people to do something, their initial response is almost always fear. If there is a challenge in front of you, a course of action that could cause you to grow and that would be helpful to people around you, but you find yourself scared about it, there's a real good chance that God is in that challenge. Take it a step further. If you're *not* facing any challenges too big for you, if it has been a while since you have felt scared, there's a real good chance that you've been sitting in the chair too long.

> *Whether it's a special assignment or just living in a fallen world, people all the time are given burdens they cannot handle.*

One day my friend Max was asked by his little granddaughter if he would like to see her run. He was surprised at this because, so far, she had not been a great walker, though she was quite comfortable with falling. So Max said of course he would like to see her run.

She lined up on one side of the room and sprinted across to the other side, directly into the refrigerator, and fell backward spread-eagle onto the floor. Concerned, Max hurried over to her and said, "Honey, you've got to learn how to stop." She looked up at him with a big grin and said, "But Grandpa, I'm learning how to run."

God makes the call, we roll the dice.

3. Reassurance

Another striking aspect of these stories: even though people almost always have an initial response of resistance, God never reacts by saying, "Oh, I can see where this would be pretty scary. Okay, never mind. I'll get somebody else."

God knows people get scared, so he makes them a promise. God said to Joshua, "Have I not commanded you? Be strong and courageous. Do not be terrified; do not be discouraged, for the LORD your God will be with you wherever you go." He said to Gideon, "The

Lord is with you, mighty warrior." No one had ever called Gideon a mighty warrior before.

Do these kinds of promises mean nothing bad will happen? To the contrary! But a man can't just sit there. The promise is that nothing can separate you from the love of God. You may suffer. You may hurt. You may die. Eventually we're all gonna die anyway. Christian journalist Greg Levoy has said that Jesus promised those who would follow him only three things: that they would be absurdly happy, entirely fearless, and always in trouble. The problem is that most of us figure that two out of three ain't bad.

4. Decision

What really matters when God calls you to do something is not whether or not you feel inadequate. Of course you will; you are inadequate. So am I. That's why God promises to go with us. What matters is your decision. Only people who say yes to challenge, demand, and risk are ever fully alive.

We went on a white-water rafting trip on the Squamish River in British Columbia.

We got around one corner known as "Devil's Elbow," and the guide said that the reason that part of the river rated level 4 (levels 5 or 6 being uninsurable) is because eight people had drowned there recently. That woke us up. We steered into a little pool, and there was a ledge fifteen or twenty feet high. She said that anyone who wanted to could climb up and jump off. She said you haven't really had an experience *of* the river until you have had an experience *in* the river.

What you couldn't see from the water was a swarm of about twenty bees up on the ledge, so you didn't want to stay there a long time. And the Squamish River is glacial runoff. All this water had been ice or snow twenty-four

> God makes the call;
> we roll the dice;
> we make the move.

hours earlier. They told us it ran at about thirty-eight degrees. Johnny and I stood there for a brief moment—a swarm of bees to the right of

us, a twenty-foot drop into frigid water in front of us. I felt very alive …
when Johnny pushed me over the edge of the cliff.

What ledge is God asking you to jump off of right now?

God makes the call; we roll the dice; we make the move.

5. Changed Life

Every time someone says yes to God, the world changes a little bit.
In the early days of the church, the legal authorities imprisoned Peter
and John for teaching about Jesus. Although the authorities tried
everything they could to intimidate Peter and John, they would not
stop talking about God. We're told that "when they saw the courage
of Peter and John and realized that they were unschooled, ordinary
men, they were astonished and they took note that these men had
been with Jesus."

Sometimes people say no. Every time you say no to God—you
change a little. Your heart gets a little harder. Your spirit dies a little.
Your addiction to comfort gets a little stronger.

It's Not the Size of the Risk That Counts

What counts as a significant risk for you will be a little different from
anyone else in the world. Research makes it clear that some people
have a strong genetic predisposition to anxiety.

Picture a bell-shaped curve: People on the far right are genetically
predisposed to be risk takers. Their brains are not very sensitive to
adrenaline and other stress modulators. They have a lot of a substance called GABA—gamma-aminobutyric acid. They require vast
amounts of risk just to keep them from feeling bored. They are drawn
to skydiving, bungee jumping, tightrope walking, alligator wrestling,
and karaoke bars.

People in the middle of the curve are set up for an average amount
of anxiety, while people on the far left are genetically predisposed to
be risk avoiders. Their brains are extremely sensitive to adrenaline,

and they have low levels of GABA. They wrestle more with worry. They may feel more anxiety about going to a party where they will have to make small talk than persons on the right side of the curve feel when they are going to jump out of an airplane. Just because you're on the right side of this bell curve does not necessarily mean you have more faith! It could just mean you have more GABA.

And just because you're on the left side doesn't mean you're spiritually inferior to the thrill seeker. This is one of the reasons Jesus said, "Don't judge." Not even yourself. Only God sees into the brains and neurons and knows what raw material we all wrestle with. The goal is for you to take what counts as a risk for *you*, one step at time, starting with where you are.

God makes the call. We roll the dice. We make the move. We begin the adventure.

Where Proof Is Possible, Faith Is Impossible

I have had the chance to see dice-rolling faith up close and personal in my father. My dad lived in the same house in Rockford, Illinois, until he went away to college. His family was 100 percent Swedish, and Swedes are not an impulsive people. He became a CPA, and CPAs as a group are usually a little more sober-minded and prudent than, say, NASCAR drivers or professional lion tamers.

When Dad was fifty years old, he got a call asking if he would be interested in moving to California to join a church staff and help them in the area of finance and administration. It was a position consistent with his wiring. He asked a number of us to pray for him about this decision, and we all agreed it seemed like it could be a life-giving move. It was a difficult decision because he had spent his entire life in one community and in one profession, and to leave all that seemed crazy. He said no.

But he could not shake the sense that he had given the wrong answer. He had a restlessness in his spirit that he could not dismiss.

Finally, one day he heard a sermon built around these words: "Where proof is possible, faith is impossible."

We would all like to be people of faith, but we would prefer a guarantee up front. I will be more generous, God, as long as you increase my revenue stream first. I will confront this injustice as long as I have the backing of the powers on top.

> *We would all like to be people of faith, but we would prefer a guarantee up front.*

Faith works the other way around. God says to the people of Israel: "I'll part the waters of the Jordan, but you have to step into the waters first. If you stand on the banks until you have proof they will part, you will be standing there for a long time."

It is the very fact that the outcome is unknown that gives courage and hope and daring meaning. If the outcome were always known ahead of time, there would be no point in playing the game. Not-knowing is our fear, and our growth.

Finally, my dad said yes. He rolled the dice. And he would tell you that the most exciting twenty years of his life have been the past twenty. He is more motivated, he is on a higher learning curve, and he is more excited about his work now than I have seen him in my entire life.

A man can't just sit there.

CHAPTER 13

PLAY
WITH GRATITUDE

What gifts am I receiving from the universe today?
And what if they don't fit or they aren't my color?
SHANTI GOLDSTEIN

Probably the single most famous speech given in the history of game players was given by a generally silent Yankee first baseman named Lou Gehrig. He stood at a microphone on a day honoring him after a fabulous career, suffering from a horrible disease that would take his life in a matter of months. He took the time to thank the vendors and ticket takers and workers who never got applause but made his job possible. And he said the words that echo still: "Today I consider myself the luckiest man on the face of the earth."

I suppose part of the reason the words move us is because they speak of gratitude in the heart of one we think would have every reason to be bitter. And because in our day we expect most people involved in big business sports to express a lot more entitlement than gratitude. We see millionaire athletes hold out against billionaire owners because "my first obligation is to my family," as if $20 million might not be enough to scrape by on.

I wonder if old Lou Gehrig, his body already falling apart from the disease that would cripple and then kill him, really did consider himself "the luckiest man." I can hardly imagine the character required to experience that much gratitude in that moment. But I know that the lucky ones, the happy ones, are the ones who play the game with gratitude.

The great secret joy of life — the prize that we think getting richer will bring us — is the ecstasy of gratitude. Gratitude is how those rich toward God — rich in *being*, not just *having* — play the game.

Gratitude:
The Ability to Experience Life as Gift

In the Civil War movie *Shenandoah*, Jimmy Stewart plays a widowed father of a large farm family. He is a cranky man with a keen sense of self-sufficiency. At the beginning of the film, he prays before each meal (because his wife made him promise to do so before she died), but it is a pretty testy prayer: "Lord, we cleared this land, we plowed it, we planted it, we harvested the crops, and we fixed the food. We worked till we were dog-boned-tired. None of this would be here if it weren't for us, but thank you anyway. Amen."

If that's the way he says "grace," you would hate to hear him complain.

Then the war comes. He loses everything. His family is ripped apart. Brothers fight against brothers. His daughter gives birth to a grandchild named Martha after his wife, but his daughter dies in childbirth. One of his sons is killed before his eyes by a frightened young sentry. His youngest son, whom he loved because the boy reminded him so much of his wife, is carried off as a prisoner of war and lost to him for many years.

Deep into the war, the remnants of the family gather around the table for a meal. Jimmy starts to pray the old prayer, "Lord, we cleared this land, we plowed it...," but he chokes up and can't go on. Suffering and loss and birth and death have shattered the illusion of self-sufficiency. Ironically, it is loss and pain that open the door to gratitude. Toward the end of the story, against all hope, Jimmy Stewart is sitting in a church when his youngest son comes home to him, comes limping down the aisle. And they stand and sing together the doxology, "Praise God from whom all blessings flow ..."

Stewart's character comes to realize that he had seen things all wrong. The reality is that his body is a gift; his children are gifts; the seeds and earth and rain and sun and growth are gifts; his work is a gift; life itself is a gift.

Then God gives one more gift: the capacity for gratitude. Gratitude is the ability to experience life as a gift. It opens us up to wonder, delight, and humility. It makes our hearts generous. It liberates us from the prison of self-preoccupation.

Earlier we looked at Jesus' story about the rich fool. One of the telling details of this story comes at the beginning where Jesus says, "The ground of a certain rich man produced a good crop." He does not say that the *man* produced the crop, because of course no man could do this. The crop was a gift. But the man did not see this. He called it "his." He was entitled.

> Gratitude is the ability to experience life as a gift. It liberates us from the prison of self-preoccupation.

Gratitude is not something we give to God because he wants to make sure we know how much trouble he went to over us. Gratitude is the gift God gives us that enables us to be blessed by all his other gifts, the way our taste buds enable us to enjoy the gift of food. Without gratitude, our lives degenerate into envy, dissatisfaction, and complaints, taking what we have for granted and always wanting more.

There is an account in the Bible about ten lepers crying out to Jesus for help. Lepers were commanded to wear torn clothes, let their hair be unkempt, and cry, "Unclean, unclean," lest anyone should have accidental contact with them. So they stood at a distance and yelled, "Jesus, Lord, have pity on us," the traditional cry of the beggar. Maybe they were hoping for a miracle. Maybe they were just hoping for some money or a little food.

Jesus' heart was moved. He told them to go show themselves to priests, which is interesting in a couple of respects. Earlier he had cleansed a leper by touching him directly. Now he commanded these ten to go show themselves *before* they had been healed, perhaps testing their faith. More than that, he commanded them to show themselves to "priests," plural. One of them was a Samaritan. Samaritans had different beliefs and different priests. Interestingly, Jesus did not tell him to get his doctrine right first. He just blessed them as he found them.

The ten left Jesus, and something happened to their broken bodies. As they went, they were healed. Skin that had been scraped raw was restored. They exchanged high fives and realized that they actually had five to exchange. They laughed, and instead of the throaty rasp that leprosy had reduced their voices to, it came out like sweet music. They leaped in the air, they landed on graceful feet, they ran for home, yelling the names of their families.

Except one. One man turned and ran back the way he had just come. He saw Jesus and fell to the ground in gratitude.

Gratitude is always an act of humility. Baptist preacher Joel Gregory writes that when the Masai tribe of West Africa express thanks, they put their foreheads on the ground and say, "My head is in the dirt." Members of another tribe express gratitude by sitting for a long while in front of the person to whom they are indebted, and then say, "I sit on the ground before you."

Ten men were cleansed. Ten were given their life back. Only one turned around. Nine ran the wrong way. Only one came back to thank the Giver for the gift. When I read the story of Jesus and the lepers, I wonder why the only grateful one was the Samaritan. I wonder if the fact that he was Samaritan and Jesus was Jewish made him that much more aware of what a gracious gift this was.

Having too much can make a person ungrateful.

The illusion of gratitude is that we will experience it more if we get new stuff that we really want. The reality is that making sure a child gets everything he or she wants is the surest way to dull the child's sense of gratitude. Dan Baker writes about how a wealthy man said that he and his rich friends call their children " 'The Royal Order of the Lucky Sperm Club.' They are born on third and think they hit a triple." Sometimes we do not realize how much we have to be grateful for until it is threatened.

Working too much makes you miss the things you ought to be grateful for.

James Dodson wrote a very moving book called *Final Rounds*, about the final months of his father's life. They were both avid golfers, and when his father had been diagnosed with a terminal illness, James took him to Scotland so they could play golf together at some of the world's most celebrated courses. At one point, James's dad asked him about his marriage and family.

> *Sometimes we do not realize how much we have to be grateful for until it is threatened.*

James's answer was evasive; he was so consumed by his work that there was little time left over. These were the words of a dying father to his son: "I wish I could slow you both down.... The danger of great ambition is that you'll work so hard, you may someday wake up and find that the things you really wanted were the things you had all along."

The Luckiest Man

The youngest of my grandmother's children married my uncle Dale. Dale was the kind of man every kid wants for an uncle because he knew more about cars than anybody in my world. When I was growing up, he held regular jobs like other dads, but he always had some car enterprise going on the side. He regularly bought and sold the most exotic cars anybody knew of.

In the sixties he owned an amphibious car that could drive on the road like a regular sports car and then navigate water. In the church where I grew up, if you brought more kids to vacation Bible school than anyone else, you would get to ride in Uncle Dale's amphi-car. He would drive you to Rock River, where, at the push of a button, the car would transubstantiate into a boat. It was like being James Bond for a day.

At various times he owned a fire engine, the world's smallest car (with an even smaller sidecar), and the first Cadillac limousine we had ever seen — complete with power windows. He owned cars that won prizes at auto shows and cars that had names you never heard of; roadsters and Model Ts; cars that were faster, bigger, louder, and stranger than anybody in Rockford had ever seen. You name the vehicle, and at one time or another, my uncle Dale owned it and drove it. I bought my first car from him when I was in grad school, a thirteen-year-old Volkswagen Super Beetle built in the late sixties.

Last fall Uncle Dale was on the roof of a warehouse trimming tree branches. His feet slipped, and he fell off the roof to the ground. A large tree limb landed on top of him. My cousin Buddy was with him. Buddy is a large man and was able to lift the limb for a moment to get one of Dale's legs out from under, but then he had to put it down.

The paramedics rushed Dale to the hospital. He was in enormous pain. Both wrists were broken, the left one in fifteen places; his left shoulder was broken; and his hip and ribs were shattered. It would have been easier to number the bones that had not broken than those that had. Dale, being Dale, gave instructions on the way to the hospital that although his overalls had been ripped, they could be mended and should not be thrown away. He also wanted to make sure someone recovered the chain saw.

By the time they got to the hospital, Dale was woozy. What no one knew at that point was that the bones were broken so badly that some of the fat was seeping out of the marrow. It's a fairly rare occurrence; hundreds of fat emboli were released and went through his bloodstream like buckshot from a shotgun, quickly making their way into his lungs and then surrounding his brain and cutting off the oxygen. It is somewhat similar to having a massive stroke. Buddy watched as his dad's eyes closed and he grew unresponsive.

By the time my aunt Becky arrived at the hospital, Dale had gone into a coma. They had to put a feeding tube down his throat to keep him nourished, and he had to be put on a ventilator or he would cease breathing. This went on day after day.

My parents flew two thousand miles to see him, and there was little doubt in anyone's mind that it was to say good-bye. One of the medical personnel told my aunt Becky that it would soon be time for some difficult decisions. If they put him on permanent life-support, he could go on living like this for months or years, and it would require a court order to stop it. On the other hand, if they simply removed the feeding tube and the ventilator, he would die.

I don't know exactly what my uncle's odds of recovery were, and I don't want to make the situation sound more dramatic than it was. From what I have read, most people who suffer from fat embolisms recover, although in most cases, those who experience one do not go into a coma. But I know the expectations of our family were very grim.

Hour after hour, day after day, Dale's wife, Becky, would sit by his bed singing and talking and praying and crying. One morning she sat by the side of his bed and said to him, "Dale, wake up. I need you to look at me. I need to tell you that I love you."

Slowly his head turned and faced in the direction of her voice. She thought that it might have been a coincidence, a reflex. So she went and sat on the other side of the bed.

"Dale, wake up. I need you to look at me. I need to tell you that I love you."

Once more, his head turned and faced the direction of the voice.

That was the beginning.

Once again, as it had over sixty years ago when he was born, the miracle of life returned to the body of my uncle Dale. His eyes opened, and he could see. His mouth opened, and he could talk. (His first words came when they removed the feeding tube from his throat—a very uncomfortable procedure.)

After many days in a coma and months of rehab, Uncle Dale went home last week. He is walking and driving again. He is not, for better and for worse, his old self again. One thing is much clearer to everyone: that life is a gift, that every day is an unpurchased miracle, every second is overtime. I do not know why life works the way it does. I do not know why some people recover and others die. I do not know why some prayers get answered and some (seem to) go unheeded. But I do know that life is a gift. I know that it is not something we earn, create, control, or sustain. I know that one truth about us is that we forget we are going to die.

The other truth is that we forget we are alive.

Some researchers have concluded that grateful people experience what they call a low threshold of gratitude. That is, just as a whisper has to reach a certain decibel level before we hear it, goodness has to reach a certain experiential level before we perceive it. And just as some of us are hard of hearing, some of us are "hard of thanking." It takes a gift of epic proportions (winning the lottery or getting a new car) before we actually feel grateful. People with a high capacity for thankfulness, on the other hand, have a low threshold for gratitude. They find that a sunset or a smile from a friend can set off a sense that they have been blessed by a gift they did not earn.

> *One truth about us is that we forget we are going to die. The other truth is that we forget we are alive.*

I cannot make myself into a grateful person. But I can open the windows of my heart to it so that when it passes through the neighborhood, I'm more likely to seize it. So I want to close this chapter with a few ways to open the window.

Keeping Track Builds Gratitude

Gratitude can be learned. Researchers Robert Emmons and Mike McCullough randomly assigned people to keep a daily diary for two weeks, either of happenings they were grateful for, of hassles, or simply of life events. Joy, happiness, and life satisfaction all rocketed up for the gratitude group.

The format they used is simple. Keep a pen and a journal or piece of paper by your bed. At night, before you go to sleep, take a few minutes to reflect on five events during the day that prompted gratitude. It could be as simple as waking up in the morning, seeing the face of someone you care for, eating a great taco, hearing words of affection from a friend, or completing a challenging assignment at work.

As you write down these events, remember that each of them came to you from the hand of God. Use them to reflect on how good God must be to give such gifts. Recognize that each of them is an expression of his love to you. Whisper to him how grateful you are for his gifts.

Hold a Gratitude Night

Researcher Martin Seligman, past president of the American Psychological Association, while trying to find a way to teach a class the difference between doing something fun and doing something altruistic, hit on the idea of a "Gratitude Night." Here are his instructions:

> Select one person from your past who has made a major difference in your life, and to whom you have never fully expressed your thanks. (Do not confound this selection with newfound romantic love, or with the possibility of future gain.) Write a testimonial just long enough to cover one page. Take your time composing this — it may take weeks.
>
> It is important to do this face-to-face, not over the phone. Do not tell the person the purpose of the visit in advance; a simple "I just wanted to see you" will suffice. Bring a laminated version of your testimonial as a gift. When all settles down, read your testimonial aloud slowly, with expression, and with eye contact. Let the other person react unhurriedly. Reminisce together about the concrete events that make this person so important to you.

Appreciate Imperfect Gifts

Next Thanksgiving you will probably sit around the table with your extended family. Maybe everyone around the table will be a model of mental health and emotional intelligence. Maybe not. Rick Warren says that every family and every group has at least one person who requires extra grace. And if you look around the table and cannot find the extra-grace-required person, it's you.

Maybe being grateful will require learning to be grateful for flawed people and imperfect gifts. Be grateful when your child attempts to make the bed, even though he or she makes it imperfectly. Be grateful when your spouse expresses affection, even though he is awkward. Be grateful that your body still moves around, even though it gets a little more wrinkled and lumpier every day.

The feeling part of gratitude is important. But don't wait to feel thankful before giving thanks. Usually the thinking and the doing lead to the emotions. C. S. Lewis once said that it's a thin line between pretending to feel something and beginning to feel it. There is a reason why the holiday is called Thanks*giving*, not Thanks*feeling*.

The apostle Paul wrote, "Wake up, O sleeper, rise from the dead, and Christ will shine on you." God says to the human race: "Wake up. I need to tell you I love you."

Every once in a while, people do wake up. When they do, what they wake up to is gratitude. Gratitude is how those who are truly rich play the game.

CHAPTER 14

FIND YOUR MISSION

This is the true joy of life; the being used for a purpose
recognized by yourself as a mighty one,
being a force of Nature rather than a feverish selfish little cloud
of ailments complaining that the world
will not devote itself to making you happy.

GEORGE BERNARD SHAW

No one gets picked for a team and then wants to sit on the bench. Nobody devotes years of service to a company with the idea that what she has done is insignificant. Nobody wants to think that at his funeral, the eulogy will declare that his life didn't matter.

We want to make a difference, and not just for ourselves. Nobody hopes that at their memorial someone will stand up and say, "He worked hard to be successful. He did a good job acquiring power and money. He was anxious and driven and self-preoccupied and polite and respectable, and he impressed a lot of people."

We want to leave the world a little changed. When it's time to go, we would like for someone to say, "My life is a little richer; my world is a little bigger; I'm a better person because this human being walked the planet awhile. He made a difference. He changed my life."

We don't want to be benchwarmers. We don't want a life on the sidelines. I don't mind losing, and I don't have to be the star, but I want to be in the game. This desire is a wonderful thing. Our hunger for significance is an indicator of who we are and why we were created. Deeper than our need for food or air or water is our need for meaning, our need to know our lives count for something. That need can get distorted by our egos. It can get sidetracked into narcissism or egotism. But we are built for meaning the way Porsches are built for speed.

The Search for Mission

Let me tell you my favorite story of one person's search for a mission, the story of Johnny the bagger. Johnny works at a grocery store. One day he went to a training event led by a speaker named Barbara Glanz. She was talking to three thousand frontline workers for a supermarket chain—truck drivers, cashiers, and stockers.

Barbara was speaking on how people can make a difference. She described how every interaction with another person is a chance to create a memory, to bless someone's life. She talked about how important it is to look for those moments. She placed on the walls, as she always does when she speaks, posters with inspiring sayings. She told some stories and then went home, but she left her phone number behind. She invited the people at the conference to give her a call if they wanted to talk more about something she said.

About a month later, Barbara received a call from one of the people at that session, a nineteen-year-old bagger named Johnny. Johnny proudly informed her that he had Down syndrome, and then he told her his story.

"Barbara, I liked what you talked about. But I didn't think I could do anything special for our customers. After all, I'm just a bagger." Then he had an idea: he decided that every night when he came home from work, he would find a "thought for the day" for his next shift. It would be something positive, some reminder of how good it was to be alive, or how much people matter, or how many gifts we are surrounded by. If he couldn't find one, he would make one up.

Every night his dad would help him enter the saying six times on a page on the computer; then Johnny would print fifty pages. He would take out a pair of scissors and carefully cut three hundred copies and sign every one.

Johnny put the stack of pages next to him while he worked. Each time he finished bagging someone's groceries, he would put his saying on top of the last bag. Then he would stop what he was doing, look the person straight in the eye, and say, "I've put a great saying in your bag. I hope it helps you have a good day. Thanks for coming here."

A month later, the store manager called Barbara. "Barbara, you won't believe what's happened here. I was making my rounds, and when I got up to the cashiers, the line at Johnny's checkout was three times longer than anyone else's. It went all the way down the frozen food aisle."

The manager got on the loudspeaker to get more checkout lines open, but he couldn't get any of the customers to move. They said, "That's okay. We'll wait. We want to be in Johnny's line." One woman came up to him and grabbed his hand, saying, "I used to shop in your store once a week. Now I come in every time I go by — I want to get Johnny's thought for the day." Johnny is doing more than filling bags with groceries; he is filling lives with hope.

There is a reason Johnny's lines are three times longer than anyone else's. Our souls need to be fed, just as our bodies do. Bodies are fed by protein and carbs; souls are fed by words. What people need from us the most is not more information. They just need words that will feed their souls. Sometimes words as simple as "thank you" or "I hope you have a really good day" can feed a soul.

> What people need from us the most is not more information. They just need words that will feed their souls.

Of course, what makes the words on the paper mean so much is who they come from. Words alone can come from a fortune cookie. When people get them from Johnny, they are reminded of the beauty of one person forgetting his own limitations and seeking to make his life a blessing to someone else. Whatever burdens Johnny carries make his gift that much brighter.

Know who the most important person in the store is?

Johnny the bagger.

A few months later, the manager called Barbara once again to tell her Johnny was transforming the whole store. He told her that when the floral department had a broken flower or unused corsage, they used to throw it away. Now they go out in the aisles, find an elderly woman or a little girl, and pin it on her. The butchers started putting ribbons on the cuts of meat they wrap up for customers. The people who make their shopping carts are trying to make carts with wheels that actually work.

And all the peoples of the grocery store will be blessed through Johnny.

If it can happen in a grocery store, it can happen anywhere.

By the way, do you know who the most important person in your family, your neighborhood, and your workplace is? You.

You can be a Johnny the bagger. What Johnny does isn't slick, complicated, or calculated. He is just a bagger expressing his heart. You can help make that happen wherever you are.

Your Mission Starts Where You Are, Not Where You Think You Should Be

Sometimes we're tempted to think that our current position/job/situation is a barrier to our mission, but, in fact, it is where it starts.

Being significant is not the same as *looking* significant. Sometimes the significance of what a person contributes doesn't get noticed until the contribution ceases. My wife is fond of telling a story about a time a husband came home from work. The house was a disaster. The baby was crying, dirty dishes were all over the counters, dirty laundry was hanging from doorknobs, the TV was blaring, beds were unmade, carpets were unvacuumed, dust was undisturbed, and dinner was uncooked. When he wanted to know what happened, his wife told him, "You know how you always ask me what I've been doing all day? Well, today I didn't do it."

Paul said, "Each one should retain the place in life that the Lord assigned to him and to which God has called him." This doesn't mean that we should never change jobs or move, of course. It does mean that if my mission cannot start here, where I am, it cannot start at all.

Jesus' idea was that when someone began to follow him, that person would become good news to everybody in the neighborhood, at the office, or in the school. His followers would become more generous and more truthful and would be "a blessing to all peoples" as God had promised Abraham.

His idea is that the gospel is good news for everybody—even people who don't believe it. As Pastor Rob Bell has written, "If the gospel isn't good news for everybody, then it isn't good news for anybody."

Your Mission Is Not about You

Jesus said, "You are the salt of the earth." But salt does not exist for itself. When is the last time you went to someone's home for a meal and said, "Man, this is great salt. Honey, how come we don't have salt like this at home? We gotta switch brands."

Salt's calling is to lose itself in something much bigger and more glorious; and then it fulfills its destiny. We were made to count. We were made to be salt. But the quest for significance is a delicate dance. If I do it *by* myself *for* myself, it's death. If I do it *with* God *for* others, it's life, because whatever I do with God for others does not go back in the box.

A century ago there was a colorful revival preacher named Billy Sunday, an ex–major leaguer who used to slide home "under the devil's tag" on the platform to show the drama of a saved soul. Billy used to say that the best thing that could happen to you was to go to one of his revivals, get saved, walk out into the street, get run over by a Mack truck, and go straight to heaven. But the "get saved and die" plan is not Jesus' Option A. His plan is for you to have a mission and a destiny starting here and now—and that mission is not about

> *If I do it by myself for myself, it's death. If I do it with God for others, it's life, because whatever I do with God for others does not go back in the box.*

building your own little kingdom, but simply about becoming rich toward God.

Your Mission Will Use Your Strengths

When God gave Moses his mission, one of the questions he asked him was, "What is that in your hand?" Moses held his staff. His staff represented his livelihood, what he knew how to do, what he was good at. It represented his resources; his flock was his wealth. It represented his security. God asked him to be willing to lay it down.

God still asks, "What is that in your hand?" What has God given you? Your gifts, your temperament, your experience, your relationships, your mind, your education — all of these help determine your mission.

God has given you what Martin Seligman calls "signature strengths." Seligman has looked across cultures and found that generally human abilities fall into certain categories:

- Wisdom and knowledge (which include abilities like curiosity, love of learning, judgment, and social intelligence)
- Courage (perseverance and integrity)
- Humanity (with capacities for kindness and the expression of mercy)
- Justice (the ability to bring about fairness and leadership)
- Temperance (qualities like self-control, prudence, humility)
- Transcendence (the appreciation of beauty, the expression of gratitude, the ability to hope, the capacity for joy)

We all have the capacity for each of these strengths. But a few of them resonate more deeply in you; they are your "signature strengths."

Seligman says we can opt for the pleasant life, the pursuit of positive feelings through psychology. We can seek the good life using our signature strengths. But the best life — the meaningful life, being on mission — is when we use our signature strengths in the service of something larger than ourselves.

Your Mission Will Use Your Weaknesses

Sometimes people think they are robbed of any chance at having a significant mission in life because of their weaknesses. In fact, the opposite is true. God never wastes a hurt. Part of what makes a human life most powerful is the struggle. No one is able to help alcoholics more than recovering alcoholics. No one can speak to those who grieve better than one who has suffered deep loss. Chuck Colson was a lawyer and a White House player, but it was not until he was a convict that he was prepared to begin Prison Fellowship.

We undervalue the role adversity plays in life. Joseph Ellis's biography of George Washington tells the story of Washington's stepson, Jackie. He was raised with all the advantages and privileges that Washington himself had lacked: his own servant, a personal tutor who resided at Mount Vernon, the newest toys, the finest clothes, his own horses and hounds for fox hunting—everything that was considered desirable for raising a successful gentleman in that culture. Ellis makes this memorable comment: "The only item Jackie was denied was adversity, and the predictable result soon began to surface," and a life was ultimately wasted.

Johnny the bagger did not have a mission *in spite of* his limitations. Rather, if he had not had those limitations, his gift would not have had the same weight. His greatest burden became his greatest gift.

Your Mission Will Be Connected to Your Deepest Dissatisfactions

What troubles you most?

For Moses, it was the oppression of his people. He hated seeing one of his brothers beaten by an Egyptian. And God used that anguish in his spirit to call Moses to lead his people to freedom.

For William Wilberforce, it was slavery. He devoted his entire life to seeing it eradicated in England, which it finally was not long before his death.

For Martin Luther King Jr., it was the injustice of a society that first enslaved and then oppressed African-Americans. So he dreamed and he preached and he marched and he organized and he boycotted, and the civil rights movement was galvanized.

For Millard Fuller, it was seeing hundreds of millions of people around the globe without a simple, decent place to live. So Millard Fuller picked up a hammer and started to build homes, and Habitat for Humanity was born.

If you want a sense of mission to burn brightly in you, spend some time feeding your divine discontent. Usually we try to avoid unpleasantness, but if you have a sense that your mission involves helping the poor, spend time around those in poverty. Allow your emotions to become deeply engaged, and carry with you that fire that things must change.

Frederick Buechner writes that generally the kind of work God calls you to is work

> (a) that you need to do and (b) that the world needs to have done. If you really get a kick out of your work, you've presumably met requirement (a), but if your work is writing cigarette ads, the chances are you've missed requirement (b). On the other hand, if your work is being a doctor in a leper colony, you have probably met requirement (b), but if you're bored and depressed by it, chances are you have not only bypassed (a) but probably aren't helping your patients much either. Neither the hair shirt nor the soft berth will do. The place God calls you to is the place where your deep gladness and the world's deep hunger meet.

For Johnny the bagger, they met at the end of a checkout line. Where do they meet for you?

Your Mission Means God Believes in You

Ned Colletti is the general manager of the Los Angeles Dodgers. He's in the talent business. Spotting talent that could make it to the big leagues — "the Show" — is his job. He has spent his whole adult life looking for talent.

Each year Colletti goes to the Dominican Republic to scout young players. Most of them, he says, have one parent. Most have never met their earthly father, and most haven't been educated past the fifth grade. Last year he saw one player in particular who had great tools but was timid because he was afraid he might fail. Ned pulled him aside and explained that failure is part of baseball — that the great Roberto Clemente, Barry Bonds, and Roger Clemens fail. He also explained that God had blessed him with a special talent that was meant solely for him. This six-foot-two-inch, two-hundred-ten-pound, gifted athlete looked at Ned with tears in his eyes and would not let go of his hand when Ned shook it as he was ready to leave.

Imagine that you're a fifteen-year-old kid in the Dominican Republic: you have never seen your father; you have no education, no money, no prospects; and you are destined for poverty. Then one day a major league scout comes along and says to you, "Follow me, and I will make you a professional baseball player."

Would you need a long time to make a decision?

Likewise, Jesus came along and called his disciples. They knew they weren't major league material. Generally, in their day, if someone was going to get to be the follower of a rabbi, it happened much earlier. Rabbis never recruited. Rabbis took applications.

Except this one. He came to fishermen and tax collectors and said, "I believe in you. What I know I will teach you. What I do you can do."

No wonder they left their nets!

Jesus sent his followers out to do what he did. And that's what he is calling you to do. He invites you to go on a mission, to come up to the Show, to play the real game. You are the salt of the earth. He can make your life a blessing.

You may feel like you're not sure you believe enough in Jesus. That's okay. He believes in you.

HAZARDS

CHAPTER 15

Beware
the Shadow Mission

If a man hasn't discovered
something that he will die for,
he isn't fit to live.
Martin Luther King Jr.

You and I were created to have a mission in life. We were made to make a difference. This is how the game is played.

But if we do not pursue the mission for which God made us, we will find a substitute. We cannot live in the absence of purpose. If we do not live our God-assigned mission, we will live what might be called a shadow mission, playing a game we were not meant to play.

A few years ago a friend talked me into going to a kind of release-the-wild-inner-hairy-warrior-within-you men's weekend. It was held in a remote and primitive quasi-military campground. I could tell you where it was, but then I'd have to kill you. We arrived in darkness. Silent men with flashlights who had watched *Apocalypse Now* once too often led us wordlessly to a processing room. Our duffel bags were searched, and all prohibited items (snacks, reading materials, signal flares) were confiscated. We were assigned numbers that were to be used instead of our names to identify us through most of the weekend. We were led blindfolded into a large hall where those of us who had arrived late or tried to smuggle contraband were instructed to stand ("Number 17. On your feet.") and tell the rest of the men in very non-faith-based language that our behavior indicated a deep-seated contempt for everyone there but ourselves.

We chanted. We marched unclad through the snow. For two days we ate bark and berries. We were sleep deprived. We howled at the moon. We sat on our haunches in a Chippewa warrior teepee/sauna purifying our souls in the glandular fellowship of sweat; thirty men evaporating in a space no more than six sane Chippewa warriors would have tried to crowd into.

We used psychodrama to reenact our quest for manhood. Usually this involved our desperate Father Hunger. We each had to wrest our masculinity away from our fathers. Our masculinity was usually represented by two oranges, which we had to pry from the relentless grasp of The Father, fighting and kicking and screaming, because manhood is not easily won. Since I have gray hair, I was chosen by an alarmingly high number of men to stand in for The Father. It was dangerous being The Father. After a while, I just started lobbing the oranges to Questing Man without even being asked. ("Here, son, take your masculinity. I want you to have it.")

It was goofy and manipulative and violated most of what I learned in clinical training about informed consent. In such situations, I will often protect myself by internally choosing to become an observer; I will pretend even to myself that I am healthy and strong and above the need for such games, and I will just be present to watch others who are needier than I am. But there were moments when I felt deep stirrings in spite of myself.

One exercise involved each man telling all the others about his sex life. Men stood and spoke about regrets, shame, failure, and hurts with the most unguarded honesty I had ever seen. One young man wept as he spoke of sleeping with a woman the previous week whose name he did not even know. Husband after husband spoke of getting up in the middle of the night to go online looking for sexually explicit sites. Even though this hurt their marriages and left them feeling empty, they couldn't seem to stop. In the New Testament, James says, "Confess your sins to each other." I wondered why this happened more transparently in a secular setting with total strangers than I have ever seen it happen in decades of church life.

The Shadow Side

The part of the discussion that has most stayed with me involved the idea that each of us has a "shadow mission." Carl Jung (whose father was a pastor) used to speak of our shadow side: those patterns of thought and action that betray our deepest values, that lead to regret and guilt. I know Jung used this in a secularized way and didn't invoke the presence of God or our need for forgiveness. But I find the image of shadow to be helpful. It describes that sense of hiddenness, vagueness, and confusion that my sin causes.

Just as we all have a mission—a way of contributing to God's kingdom that we were designed and gifted for—we also have what might be called a shadow mission. My shadow mission is what I will do with my life if I drift on autopilot. It consists of the activities toward which I will gravitate if I allow my natural temptations and selfishness to take over. Everybody has a shadow mission.

By way of illustration, one of the staff members told us, "My shadow mission is to watch TV and masturbate while the world goes to hell." A round of nervous laughter swept across the circle of men.

"I'm going to say it one more time," the man said, "only this time I want you to listen and not laugh." And then he said it again: "My shadow mission is to watch TV ..."

This time the silence was sobering. Each of us was thinking the same thing: how easily any of our lives can slide into such a self-centered, trivial pursuit. He wasn't tempted to be Adolf Hitler or Saddam Hussein. The man would have fought against that kind of outright evil. It was the banality of his shadow mission that made it so possible.

Partly our shadow missions are shaped by our culture. The rich fool in Jesus' story had a clear shadow mission: build bigger barns and lay up plenty of goods for many years. Take life easy: eat, drink, and be merry.

> *Just as we all have a mission—a way of contributing to God's kingdom that we were designed and gifted for— we also have a shadow mission.*

Frodo's mission in The Lord of the Rings trilogy is to be the ring bearer, to bless Middle Earth by destroying the ring in the fires of doom. The hardest part of his mission is not defeating external enemies. The hardest part is renouncing the shadow mission of choosing to claim the ring for himself and seeking his own power and glory.

Being clear on my own shadow mission and naming it is enormously helpful, because when I see it for what it is, I realize how much I do not want to devote my life to it. At the end of the game, our shadow missions all spell the same result: despair.

Shadow Mission in the Bible

The book of Esther is, among other things, a book of missions and shadow missions and how they are woven into the great mission of God. At the beginning of the book, King Xerxes is having a party. His kingdom extended from Asia Minor all the way down into Africa, then across to northern parts of India. He was not an admirable character. The writer uses skill, satire, and exaggeration to give us a picture of an ostentatious king who wants to show off his greatness but in fact has no inner strength of character and constantly needs other people to make up his mind.

The book opens with the king at a 180-day banquet (three banquets are described in the first chapter alone; one way to divide the book up is as a series of banquets) — six months of serious partying. Following that feast, he threw another party for the whole capital, open to common people. The people drank "by flagons" without restraint, no designated drivers. On the seventh day, "when the king was merry with wine," he sent for the queen, Vashti. He had been showing off his possessions; now he wanted to show off his ultimate possession.

What do you think he wanted to show them about her? Her brains — come and do math problems? Her personality — have a lively discussion about the decline of the Babylonian Empire?

No, he wanted Vashti to come "in order to display her beauty to the people and nobles, for she was lovely to look at."

Then an extraordinary thing happened. She said thanks very much but she would just as soon take a pass and stay home to wash her hair.

You would think the king might have realized what an awkward position he had put her in, but you'd be wrong. "Then the king became furious and burned with anger."

Vashti was threatening his shadow mission of impressing a nation. He looked weak. So he turned to "experts in matters of law and justice"—their version of the Supreme Court. He couldn't control the queen, so he made this a matter of state: "What am I going to do about my wife? She washed her hair, and I can't do a thing with her." Xerxes wasn't concerned with justice; he just wanted to appear to be in control. He was doing impression management.

Xerxes' supreme court advised him to pass an edict that Vashti not be allowed to come before the king anymore (which probably didn't break her heart since that was her crime in the first place) and that he get a new queen.

Xerxes liked this idea. He turned to his "personal attendants" for advice on the search. This was not the Supreme Court; these were his bodyguards, high-testosterone young men who gave him their ideas of what to look for in a new queen. Want to guess their number one criterion? They suggested he hold a "Miss Media and Persia" beauty contest in which each province—127 in all—would contribute one finalist to the royal harem. Then each contestant would go through rigorous beauty treatments, the ancient version of extreme makeovers. In the end, "the girl who pleased the king" would become the ultimate trophy wife.

One of contestants was a young Jewish girl named Esther, adopted and raised by her cousin, Mordecai. We're told she was "lovely in form and features." She made it through the prelims and was one of the finalists selected to go before the king. We are not told what Esther's dreams for her life had been. We do not know whether she volunteered for this contest or was drafted. At the outset, the story sounds a little like Cinderella or Snow White. Maybe the glamour and opportunities of being queen were deeply exciting for her. Or maybe the prospect of being married to the king was frightening. In any case, whatever dreams she had had for her life to this point had been wildly interrupted. Even more certainly, she had no idea what the future would hold for her. Neither do you or I.

> *Esther had no idea what the future would hold for her. Neither do you or I.*

Esther began to prepare to go in to the king. Before a girl's turn came to go in to King Xerxes, she had to complete twelve months of beauty treatments prescribed for the women, we are told; six months with oil of myrrh, and six months with perfumes and cosmetics (thankfully liposuction and silicone hadn't been invented yet). This was a lot of pressure for a first date. If someone is not attracted to you after twelve months of prep time, it's probably not going to happen.

Esther, a model of modesty and restraint, won the contest and was named the new queen. The king threw another party. It looked like Esther's mission was to be arm candy for the most powerful man on earth — that is, until her life was interrupted a second time.

"*For such a time as this . . .*"

It turns out that the king's chief of staff, Haman, had been mortally offended by Esther's guardian, Mordecai, because Mordecai would not bow in his presence and "pay him honor." Haman was obsessed with power, and one tiny corner of rebellion could not be overlooked. He decided to get revenge by destroying all the Jews in the kingdom; he duped and bribed the clueless king into decreeing the genocide of the Israelites.

When word of Haman's treachery reached Mordecai, he realized that there was only one person in the empire in a position to intervene with the king to seek to save all of Israel: the pageant winner. God's plan for a redemptive community was placed in the slender hands of a beauty queen named Esther. God revealed his mission to Esther, as he often does to you and me, at least partly through the words of a wise and trusted spiritual friend. You must go to the king, Mordecai told her.

Esther was not trained for this moment. She had been taught that her value to the king was her face and body. For twelve months she had been trained to try to anticipate and then please his every desire. It was a capital offense for someone to approach the king unsummoned—and the king hadn't even asked for Esther for a month. The honeymoon was over, the harem was full, and Esther did not have a devoted husband. Esther knew what had happened to Vashti. It would be suicide to take on Haman, the real power behind the throne.

The queen had good reason to take a pass. And many friends would stop the conversation there. But not Mordecai. He told Esther that to settle for being a wealthy, pampered beauty queen was her shadow mission. Her true mission was to use courage and savvy to save her people. He spoke the words that would echo in her mind until her final day: "Who knows but that you have come to royal position for such a time as this?" The fate of a whole nation, the fate of the people of God, rested in her hands.

Esther had not been brought to this point in her life for the sake of accumulating an exquisite wardrobe and precious gems. She had not been brought to this point to become the most desirable woman in the kingdom. Safety, security, fame, attractiveness—these were not her mission. They were her shadow mission. Her mission was to be part of God's plan to redeem the world. And so it is no accident that she was where she was. "Who knows" said Mordecai, "but that you have come to royal position for such a time as this?"

Discovering what is needed to fulfill the meaning of your life is not the same thing as being successful, and it is never easy. But deep in our souls we know an easy mission is not what we were made for. It will not thrill us. No one ever went to see a movie called *Mission Not So Difficult*.

Esther asked to have three days of fasting and prayer before she approached the king. "When this is done, I will go to the king, even though it is against the law," she said. And then she responded with words that were as magnificent in their courage as Mordecai's were in their challenge: "And if I perish, I perish."

There were depths in Esther that even she did not suspect — as perhaps there are in you. Some time ago somebody at a Mattel factory messed up, and voice boxes intended for Barbie dolls ended up getting installed in GI Joes, and vice versa. Hundreds of kids were shocked to hear Joe say, "Let's go shop till we drop."

> There were depths in Esther that even she did not suspect — as perhaps there are in you.

And an equal number of young girls heard Barbie bark out, "Hit the ground now. Hard, hard, hard." Xerxes thought he had married Barbie, but he ended up with GI Joe.

On the third day, Esther put on royal robes and stood in the inner court waiting for the king. Imagine what went through her mind as she waited. *Life or death?*

The king saw Esther. He reached out his scepter, the indication of royal favor. She would live for another day. He asked, "What is your petition? It will be given you. And what is your request? Even up to half the kingdom, it will be granted."

Esther understood this is the kind of thing a king said when he was in a good mood, but it wasn't to be taken literally. If she had actually asked for half the kingdom, things would have changed radically. This was more or less king talk for, "Would you like to hold the remote control tonight?"

Esther couldn't blurt out, "I'd like to have you revoke the unalterable law of the Medes and Persians, spare my people, and put down your chief of staff." So she said, "I'm having a party. You and Haman come."

The king had never turned down a party in his life. And he had such a good time at Esther's party that he asked her a second time about her petition. She in turn invited him to a second party and told him she would ask him then. Esther was now showing remarkable skill. By coming, the king had almost already agreed to her request.

The Soul Is Not Fed by Shadows

Haman was of course excited to be included in all of this. That night he boasted to his wife and friends about "his vast wealth, his many sons, and all the ways the king had honored him." But then he complained, "All this gives me no satisfaction as long as I see that Jew Mordecai sitting at the king's gate." Haman's shadow mission was *more*: more wealth, more power, more recognition. But the soul cannot be fed by shadows. It was not enough. It never is. His wife advised him to have a gallows built seventy-five feet high and have Mordecai hung on it. "This suggestion delighted Haman, and he had the gallows built."

That same night, the king couldn't sleep. He asked his servant to read to him (as king he figured he didn't have to read himself to sleep) from the annals of the king. "Read that book about me," he ordered.

And they read to him the story of how a man named Mordecai once saved his life. When the king asked what recognition Mordecai had received for his good deed, his servant replied that Mordecai had never been honored. At this moment, Haman arrived to ask the king to hang Mordecai, knowing nothing of the account the servant had just read to the king. The king preempted him with a question: "What should be done for the man the king delights to honor?"

Sure that he must be that man, Haman told the king that the man should be dressed in royal robes and ride a royal horse led by a royal official, and for good measure, even the horse should wear a crown. "This is what is done," Haman said (*nudge, nudge, wink, wink*), "for the man the king delights to honor!"

Imagine the moment. "Okay," said the king. "The man is Mordecai. Haman, you walk his horse through the city; you tell everybody he's the man I delight to honor."

From here on out it was all downhill for Haman. Esther held another banquet and engaged the king with courage and skill. She told him that she and her people were to be destroyed.

"Where is the man who has dared to do such a thing?" asked the king.

"The adversary and enemy is this vile Haman," the queen replied.

Haman ended up being hung on the very gallows built for Mordecai.

The king needed a new chief of staff. Esther arranged that as well: "Esther appointed [Mordecai] over Haman's estate." Esther then returned to the king and reminded him that the edict that spelled death for her people was still in effect. The king gave her his ring and said, "Write another decree in the king's name in behalf of the Jews as seems best to you, and seal it with the king's signet ring—for no document written in the king's name and sealed with his ring can be revoked." This new decree gave the Jews the right to defend themselves against Haman's terrorists. And the people of Israel were so favored, we're told, that "many people of other nationalities became Jews."

No Accident

What does this story have to tell us about our missions and our shadows? First of all, it says that perhaps where you are today is no accident. Who knows but that you have come to your position for such a time as this?

Esther did not set out to be queen, but once she was on the throne, she had to decide between a shadow mission of safety, wealth, and power and her God-given mission of saving her people. On the other hand, Haman could have used his position to promote justice but gave in instead to the shadow mission of self-idolatry and cruelty. The king could have embraced a mission of generosity but instead settled for a shadow mission of shallow pleasure.

What is your position? Maybe it involves your job, your marriage, your tasks as a parent, or your friendships. Maybe your position includes going to school. Maybe it involves the neighborhood where you live, or volunteering, or your church. One thing is for sure: *this* is your time. Not some other situation. Not tomorrow or yesterday. We are often tempted to think that we are treading water right now, waiting for some other time, some more important position. You don't get to choose your time; your time chooses you. You are where and who you are for a reason.

> *You don't get to choose your time; your time chooses you. You are where and who you are for a reason.*

The story also causes us to consider who plays the role of Mordecai in our lives. If Esther had not had a Mordecai, perhaps she never would have understood her mission. Without his challenge, she might not have embraced it. No one could achieve her mission but her, but she did not do it alone.

Who is your Mordecai? Who knows you well enough to help you identify what God is calling you to do? Who loves you enough to challenge you when you want to shrink back?

Jesus and the Shadow

Did Jesus face a shadow mission? I think so. We are told by the writer of Hebrews that he was tempted "in every way" like us but was without sin. For Jesus, the shadow mission was to be Messiah without suffering. The great New Testament scholar F. F. Bruce writes, "Time and again the temptation came to Him from many directions to choose some less costly way of fulfilling that calling than the way of suffering and death, but he resisted it to the end and set his face steadfastly to accomplish the purpose for which He had come into the world." In the desert, Satan tempted Jesus to achieve his mission without hunger, without pain ("His angels ... will lift you up in their hands"), and without opposition ("[All the kingdoms of the world] I will give you").

Later on when Jesus told the disciples he must suffer and die, Peter tried to convince him that his suffering was unnecessary. This was the same shadow mission, and that is why Jesus rebuked Peter so sharply, saying, "Get behind me, Satan!" All the way to the garden of Gethsemane, Jesus wrestled with this, praying, "Take this cup from me." Jesus himself had to enter in to our desperate "Father hunger." "My God, my God, why have you forsaken me?" he cried from the cross. His great victory was his victory over the temptation of his shadow mission, a Messiah without a cross. And his victory gave his followers courage to renounce their own shadow missions.

Esther's story reminds us that there is a law that is unalterable; there is a will that will not be turned, but it isn't the law of the Medes and Persians. How is it that of all the women in the empire, a Jewish girl named Esther became queen? How is it that of all the people in the empire, Mordecai was the one who saved the king from assassination? How is it that the king should have insomnia on the very night Haman had built a gallows for Mordecai? How is it that of all stories, the one read to the king was of Mordecai saving his life? How is it that Haman, the scheming murderer, became victim of his own schemes and that Mordecai, his intended victim, became instead his replacement?

Even in exile, where there is no Jerusalem, no temple, and no Sanhedrin, God is present. He is still Master of the Board. To miss out on the mission he gives is to spend our entire lives trying to win the wrong game. Even though God is unseen by Esther, his purpose is certain. He is always present with her.

As he is with you and me.

CHAPTER 16

TWO CHEERS
FOR COMPETITION

Eternity is long.
Especially toward the end.

WOODY ALLEN

Laura Hillenbrand, in her prize-winning book *Seabiscuit*, writes about Seabiscuit's greatest moment in his race against War Admiral. War Admiral was the heavy favorite, a Triple Crown winner who had obliterated all the horses he ran against. Seabiscuit's longtime jockey, Red Pollard, could not ride him because of an injury, so he gave his replacement, George "The Iceman" Woolf, advice on how to run the race that defied conventional wisdom. Have Seabiscuit jump out to the lead, Pollard told Woolf, but then when War Admiral launches his final drive for the wire, do something completely unexpected; let him catch up.

This went against all common sense, but Pollard said it was a case of horse psychology. "Once a horse gives Seabiscuit the old look-in-the-eye," Pollard said, "Seabiscuit begins to run to parts unknown.... War Admiral has speed, good speed; speed when unopposed. But with Seabiscuit, you could kill him before he'd quit.... It's not in his feet, George. It's in his heart."

The crowd assembled, the whole country stopped work to form the largest radio audience that had ever been assembled, and in the White House, FDR put off a cabinet meeting to listen in. The bell rang and the race began. Seabiscuit jumped into the lead. Coming into the backstretch, Woolf pulled back ever so gently on the reins. War Admiral drew even with Seabiscuit, both horses' strides falling

181

in perfect synchronization. Woolf could see Seabiscuit looking directly into the eyes of his rival. His ears flattened to his head. Woolf felt a subtle hesitation in War Admiral, a wavering. He leaned low and called into Seabiscuit's ear to give him everything he had. War Admiral began sliding from Seabiscuit's side "as if gravity were pulling him backward." Seabiscuit's ears flipped up. Seabiscuit had broken him. Woolf made a small motion with his hand to War Admiral's jockey, Charles Kurtsinger, saying, "So long, Charley," a phrase he coined that would be used by jockeys for decades. Seabiscuit ran into history, winning by four lengths, and pandemonium broke out behind him.

Call it drive, heart, or the will to win — whatever you call it, we are deeply moved by the display of competitive greatness. When a competitor prepares his mind and body through rigorous training, then stares the challenge of his life in the eye and reaches down deep within himself to give his last ounce of effort to the battle, it touches something visceral in everyone who watches. It is Joe Montana jogging to the huddle with two minutes left in the Super Bowl, down five points with eighty yards to go. It is Tiger Woods up by one stroke on the eighteenth hole at Augusta. It is my grandmother with a pair of dice in her hand and Boardwalk on the line at the Monopoly table. Not only do we love to watch it, we hope that some of this spirit might be in us as well.

> Merely winning doesn't mean we have always achieved our inner excellence, and losing doesn't mean we have neglected it.

We play games to win. But merely winning doesn't mean we have always achieved this inner excellence, and losing doesn't mean we have neglected it. There is a score inside us, a measure of determination and heart and courage under pressure that matters more than the points on the board. Winning and losing apart from this inner score do not matter much.

We play games to test ourselves. What makes a game a game instead of simply a pastime is that it poses a problem, a challenge to be overcome. I may think of myself as competing against other people, yet, in a sense, I need my opponent because he pushes me to levels of effort and excellence that I otherwise never would reach. Always, the real contest is to see if I can offer my best, to see if I can run and not give up in the face of a great demand. The ancient Greeks loved games as opportunities to test themselves, to develop that excellence of mind, body, and spirit that they called *arate*, that could extend to overcoming challenges in every area of life.

In my business, in my marriage, in my family, in my faith, and at school, as I'm seeking to master a new discipline, I resolve to strive. Something about competition touches this resolve in us, calling it forth. War Admiral comes up and gives you the old look-in-the-eye, and you dig down deeper than you knew you could. "So long, Charley." This resolve is essential to human growth, glory, and greatness.

Competitive greatness is a love for the battle, because it is in the struggle and the challenge that you are offered the opportunity to be your best when your best is required. Competitive drive can get distorted, as we saw in chapter 3 on keeping score. That's why this chapter's title only gives competition two cheers instead of three.

The apostle Paul warned about the dangers of ego and misguided ambition as much as anyone. But the drive of a runner to win the race was one of his favorite pictures of the life of faith. "One thing I do: Forgetting what is behind and straining toward what is ahead, I press on toward the goal to win the prize for which God has called me heavenward in Christ Jesus." "I have fought the good fight, I have finished the race, I have kept the faith." "Do you not know that in a race all the runners run, but only one gets the prize? Run in such a way as to get the prize."

The Alternative

We play the game to test ourselves. Gordon MacDonald wrote about a comment a relative made after his mother died: "She never really finished anything she started. When things got difficult, she would walk away." As he reflected on her life, Gordon saw a pattern of unfinished projects and unrealized dreams. And he thought about this pattern in his own life. It is a sobering thing, he wrote, to realize that you have a quitter's gene in your DNA.

Finishing school will be difficult, so you decide to bail. Dieting is boring, so you settle for body-by-Pillsbury Doughboy. Pulling the marriage together would take effort, so you let it drift apart. Mastering finances would take discipline, so the bills pile up. Sticking with a job is tedious, so you look for something more glamorous. War Admiral comes down the stretch, and you look away.

I thought about the "quitter's gene" a lot. I had never thought of myself as a quitter. But the more I reflected, the more I realized that I had a kind of expectation that my life should not be painful or difficult. I was with a good friend of mine from college days recently, and he said that one of his observations of me when we were in college was that I had not experienced a time of difficult struggle. In retrospect I think that was because I tried to engage only in activities in which I felt like I could shine. I sought to avoid areas in which I would have to practice, in Eugene Peterson's phrase, a "long obedience in the same direction."

Many years later I had a season in my work during which it felt like all sorts of things were going wrong. We had had a fractious congregational meeting over a staff member who was leaving. Another key staff member had resigned over difficult personal issues, and a partner in ministry was moving across the country. I felt alone and ineffective. I was driving to church to make an announcement when the thought occurred to me, *This is one of those moments when I get to choose persistence in the face of looming obstacles.* It was not a time for me to waste energy by wondering if I should be somewhere else. It was not a time for me to question whether I could do it. This was — for me — one of those moments when War Admiral was giving me the old look-in-the-eye, and I would decide whether the quitter's gene was dominant or recessive. And it was strangely liberating for me to say to God in that moment, "I'll just keep running this course. I don't know that I can win, but I will run the best I can."

Remember What You Run For

"Everyone who competes in the games goes into strict training. They do it to get a crown that will not last; but we do it to get a crown that will last forever. Therefore I do not run like a man running aimlessly; I do not fight like a man beating the air." If you play well enough, whatever your game, there's a place for you in a hall of fame. There are today not just dozens, or scores, but thousands of halls of fame. Most colleges have them. There is a hall of fame for billiards players, chess competitors, and Scottish sports stars. There is a Barbed Wire Hall of Fame, a Kansas Oil and Gas Hall of Fame, a Military Intelligence Hall of Fame. (Is this one a good idea? If you're a great spy, do you want the whole world to know?) The only hall of fame waiting to be established is a hall of fame to recognize the world's greatest halls of fame.

Hebrews 11 serves as a kind of spiritual hall of fame. Picture a wall filled with plaques featuring the names and faces of the heroes of the faith: Noah,

> *When the game is over, the spiritual hall of fame is the one that will matter. And you can be in this hall.*

Abraham, Moses, Rahab, Gideon, and others. They were the champions who rejoiced in running the course. The writer speaks of how each one of them faced obstacles that would have offered a thousand excuses to quit. But they did not. Instead, their difficulties fired a drive deep within them. They looked War Admiral in the eye and refused to quit: destitute, persecuted, mistreated—"the world was not worthy of them.... They were all commended for their faith, yet none of them received what had been promised." When the game is over, this is the hall of fame that will matter. And you can be in this hall.

The Dash

The writer of Hebrews goes on to say that now it's our turn. "Since we are surrounded by such a great cloud of witnesses"—such champions—"let us run with perseverance the race marked out for us." Imagine walking through this spiritual hall of fame. You read the names. You scan the faces. You see on every plaque those two dates that indicate when the person's race began and when it ended, with the little dash in between. Then you come to your plaque. What does it say?

I would like to invite you to personalize this part of the book. Under this paragraph are some empty lines. Put your name in the upper one. Below that you will find two blanks. They are the bookends of your life. On the left line, write the year of your birth. (No one's looking, so you can be honest about it.) The date on the right is still a mystery, so I have put in a question mark. And in between the two blanks is a dash.

You had no say at all in that number on the left. You arrived on this planet one day without being consulted ahead of time. Ready or not, here you came. You did not get to vote on your parents, your birthplace, your family order, or your DNA. All of these were chosen for you. You were made the bearer of a human soul, created in the image of God, destined for an eternal existence.

You may be very happy about having entered the world, or you may feel that your life is a crushing burden. But you should know this: God is very pleased that you exist. He "knit you together in your mother's womb." That year when you were born is one of his favorite years.

One day the question mark on the right will be replaced by a number as well. We don't have much say about that number either. This is part of what gives life its urgent value. We have one shot at it.

That brings us to the great question: What are you going to do with your dash? What will you do with the turns you get to play the game? That little dash is yours to spend: to shape character, to give allegiance, to choose hope or cynicism, to seize initiative or resign in passivity; to grow or stagnate, to be known or to hide.

And the range of what is possible in one life is staggering: Adolf Hitler, Mother Teresa, Martin Luther King Jr., Attila the Hun, my grandmother—each of these was given a single dash.

And now—ready or not—you have been given a turn. The bell has sounded. It's your race now. What will you do with your dash?

CHAPTER 17

MORE WILL NEVER BE ENOUGH

Men have succeeded in accumulating
a greater mass of objects,
but the joy in the world has grown less.

FYODOR DOSTOYEVSKY

In an old black-and-white movie named *Key Largo*, a rapacious gangster played by Edward G. Robinson, whose life is filled with violence and deceit, holds a family hostage. Someone asks him what drives him to lead this kind of life — what he wants. His face clouds over; he is not a reflective man and doesn't know how to answer the question. One of the hostages, played by Humphrey Bogart, suggests an answer: "I know what you want. You want *more*."

Robinson's face brightens. "Yeah, that's it. That's what I want. I want *more*." His character believes the myth of more, the myth that one day more will be enough. If we believe this myth, we spend our lives looking for The Next Thing. It might be a car, or a promotion, or the love of a beautiful woman. It might be, depending on our age, an iPod, or a Lamborghini, or Tickle Me Elmo. We keep hoping that The Next Thing will be IT — the source of true satisfaction for our souls.

And for a few minutes, or perhaps days, we experience true soul satisfaction. Then it wears off. It always wears off. But we always want more of the board and to be its master.

We have already looked at the importance of playing the game with gratitude, but the desire for more deserves a chapter all its own.

For even the most grateful person among us still knows the ache for more. And I believe our hunger for more has something important to tell us about our destiny, which we will get to after we consider where the road called "more" leads.

The Unscratchable Itch

Michael Drosnin wrote a book about a man whose name became synonymous with the hunger for more. He wanted more wealth, so he built one of the greatest financial empires of his day. He wanted more pleasure, so he seduced or paid for the most glamorous women money could buy. He wanted more adventure, so he set airspeed records and designed, built, and piloted the world's most unique aircraft. He wanted more power, so he acquired political clout that was the envy of senators. He wanted more glamour, so he crashed Hollywood, owned studios, courted stars.

Drosnin tells how this man's life ended:

> He was a figure of gothic horror, ready for the grave. Emaciated, only 120 pounds stretched out over his six-foot-four-inch frame ... thin scraggly beard that reached midway onto his sunken chest, hideously long nails in grotesque yellowed corkscrews.... Many of his teeth were black, rotting stumps. A tumor was beginning to emerge from the side of his head ... innumerable needle marks.... Howard Hughes was an addict. A billionaire junkie.

Here's the question: if Howard Hughes had pulled off one more deal, made one more million, tasted one more thrill, would it have been enough?

She was the most adulated of women. Every woman envied her; every man wanted her. She had beauty, money, wealth, and so much fame that on the day I write this — four decades after her death — hundreds of her personal possessions are being auctioned off in

Southern California. But Marilyn Monroe died alone, died of her own hand.

Here's the question: if she had had one more hit movie, one more magazine cover, one more sexual relationship with a powerful man, would it have been enough?

I love my wife. But here's another question: if she were to take a credit card and go to Neiman Marcus for one day of unlimited shopping, acquire every shoe she liked, every purse she fancied, every dress she admired, and every piece of jewelry her heart desired, would it be enough?

I have said it before: we'll never know.

> We are all against materialism. We don't want to be materialistic! We just want more.

We are all against materialism. In a recent extensive survey, 89 percent of the Americans who were polled said the United States is too materialistic. By sheer coincidence, almost exactly the same percentage of us said we wanted even more for ourselves. We don't want to be materialistic! We just want more.

My grandmother understood about the myth of more. We lived next door to a vacant field overgrown with shrubs and trees, a perfect place to play. In June, with the heat and sweltering humidity, it was also a perfect breeding ground for an insect called a chigger. Think of a mosquito on steroids.

They would attack in squadrons. They loved the warmest and moistest places on the body. The itch was irresistible. For a few days I would try to manage the itch by scratching. It felt wonderful for a few moments, but the itch wasn't defeated. It just went away to work out for a while and come back stronger than ever.

I remember once going to my grandmother, who pulled out something called calamine lotion, which she spread over all the chigger bites with a cotton swab. And when she did, she explained to me the Law of the Itch: "No one ever made an itch go away by getting really good at scratching."

The King of More

Maybe no one ever got better at scratching than Solomon. The book of Ecclesiastes is devoted to his search for The Next Thing. He was in a unique position to do this search. He had wealth, power, and abilities that exceeded anyone else alive. The phrase "I devoted myself to ..." keeps coming up in his book. He did not dabble. He writes, "I thought in my heart, 'Come now, I will test you with pleasure to find out what is good.'"

Solomon threw such lavish parties that one day's food supply for the palace included thirty head of cattle, one hundred sheep, five hundred bushels of flour and meal, deer, gazelles, and exotic poultry.

He surrounded himself with beauty: parks, gardens, vineyards, and houses.

He constructed a palace so magnificent it defied description. Solomon's home took a construction crew of 150,000 thirteen years to build. It was a really nice house.

He liked music, and since there were no CDs back then, he collected an orchestra of every known instrument and drafted all the finest singers in his day to serenade him at mealtimes.

He accumulated one thousand wives and concubines. He was supposed to be the smartest guy in the world, yet he collected a thousand wives.

He indulged every appetite. "I denied myself nothing my eyes desired; I refused my heart no pleasure."

He tried out-achieving everyone. He built his nation up to the greatest prominence it would know. He earned more than twenty-five tons of gold a year. His verdict: "I turned my head and saw yet another wisp of smoke on its way to nothingness: a solitary person ... working obsessively late into the night, compulsively greedy for more and more, never bothering to ask, 'Why am I working like a dog, never having any fun? And who cares?' More smoke. A bad business." "All man's efforts are for his mouth, yet his appetite is never satisfied." "Whoever loves money never has money enough."

Solomon says, "Go ahead and try. You can walk down that road as far as you want to. I did." Know this: the smartest guy who ever lived went farther down that road than you ever will and concluded that none of that was IT. Nothing had brought him lasting soul satisfaction.

What Lies behind the Itch?

Talk-show host Dennis Prager wrote about an ad he read for a sex therapist in Los Angeles: "If you're not completely satisfied with your sex life, give us a call." The more he thought about it, the more he was struck by the brilliance of the ad, all because of two words: "completely satisfied." Who is ever completely satisfied with anything? Imagine these ads:

> If you're not *completely satisfied* with your spouse, give us a call.
> If you're not *completely satisfied* with your body, give us a call.
> If you're not *completely satisfied* with your church, give us a call.

We are completely satisfied with nothing.

Why are we completely satisfied by nothing on earth? Maybe it's because we are too demanding. Maybe the answer is to bank our desires, settle for what life gives, and try to keep ourselves from wanting.

Or maybe it's because we were made for something earth does not have to offer and we're playing life's game in a way it wasn't designed to be played.

The Hedonic Treadmill

When we try to be happy by getting more, we live on what is sometimes called the "hedonic treadmill." This means we rapidly adapt to and take for granted acquisitions and achievements in our life. When we acquire what we want, we feel a little thrill of gratification. Before we get it, we feel a lack. We think that the acquisition will make that

sense of lack go away, but, like Lassie, dissatisfaction always comes
back home. The only "more" we end up receiving is more wanting.

We suffer from an apparently limitless capacity to take what used
to be "wants" and turn them into "needs." We live in what social
theorist Greg Easterbrook calls "abundance denial," in which millions
of men and women construct elaborate mental rationales for considering themselves materially deprived and, in so doing, only succeed
in increasing their unhappiness. Below are items rated as necessities
by Americans in 1970 as compared to 2000:

	1970	2000
Second car	20%	59%
Second TV	3%	45%
More than one phone	2%	78%
Car air-conditioning	11%	65%
Dishwasher	8%	44%

In a Gallup poll, the respondents, on average, said that 21 percent
of Americans are rich. But only 0.5 percent said they were rich. Everybody thinks he needs one thing to make himself rich: more.

We suffer from a phenomenon called "reference anxiety," more
often referred to as "keeping up with the Joneses." We don't ask if our
homes or cars meet our needs. We ask if they are nicer than those of
our neighbors. We work like crazy to make it so. But what do you do
when the Joneses refinance?

We suffer from the effects of entitlement. If I think long enough
about something I really want, my mind can convince itself that I
deserve to have it, that somehow my rights have been violated if I do
not have it. This has led to a proliferation of law suits, because when
people don't get something, they want to sue someone.

The San Francisco Giants were sued for passing out Father's Day
    gifts to men only.

A psychology professor sued for sexual harassment because of the
presence of mistletoe at a Christmas party.

A psychic was awarded $986,000 when a doctor's CAT scan
impaired her psychic abilities.

I wonder about this last one. If she really was a psychic, shouldn't she
have known not to go to that doctor?

Study after study shows the shockingly low correlation between
wealth and happiness. One of the most fascinating in this regard is a
study of lottery winners done by Dr. Ronnie Janoff Bulman and her
colleagues. They compared twenty-two winners of major lotteries to
twenty-two average people and also to twenty-nine victims of sudden
paralysis. Over time the lottery winners reverted to their pre-lottery
levels of happiness (or depression) and, in fact, wound up no happier
than twenty-two control subjects. They even lost much of their ability to extract joy from small pleasures.

The paralysis victims, on the other hand, were not nearly as unhappy as might be expected. Once they got over the shock of their
misfortune, they were actually more capable of experiencing joy from
small pleasures than the lottery winners. And although it's hard to
believe, they were actually more optimistic about their prospects for
future happiness than the lottery winners.

One of the nation's leading researchers on happiness, Dr. Ed Diener, interviewed forty-nine of the country's wealthiest people. Eighty
percent of them agreed that wealth could make people unhappy.

We suffer from impaired judgment. Investors are fond of talking
about one of the strangest speculative booms in history, a seventeenth-century Dutch frenzy called *Tulpenwoerde*, or tulipmania. The
whole country hoarded tulips in the belief that their price would rise
indefinitely. At its height, whole family fortunes were squandered on
a single bulb; one rare bulb was given as full payment for a successful
brewery.

A shoemaker in The Hague was able to grow the rarest of beau-
ties: a black tulip. He was visited by some growers from Haarlem who

bought his treasure for 1,500 florins. They immediately dropped his flower to the ground and stomped it to pieces; they too possessed a black tulip and were determined to have the only one. They told him they would have paid any price — up to 10,000 florins for his. The heartbroken cobbler is said to have died of chagrin.

When the price levels cracked, the entire economic life of Holland crumbled. Lawsuits were so numerous the courts couldn't handle them. The Dutch have never been quite so free with their money ever since.

The Deeper Problem

We suffer from something even more dangerous. Ever wonder what makes the myth of more so strong? A clue lies in a warning the apostle Paul gives about our desires for more. He says to beware of greed, "which is idolatry." In other words, our problem isn't just that we want more.

We are not just physical stuff; we are spiritual beings. And our deepest hunger is spiritual. We hunger for meaning. We hunger for love. We hunger for redemption.

The condition underneath all my wanting is that what I really want is God, and for creation to be set right by God, beginning with that little piece of creation that is my body and soul. But my wanting gets distorted. I. Howard Marshall writes that the rich fool in Jesus' story isn't covetous just because he wants a pleasant retirement. His folly is that he believes the storage of grain — building a 401(k), funding an IRA — solves the problem of his human existence. He worships at the shrine of the bulging barn.

> Our problem isn't just that we want more. We are not just physical stuff; we are spiritual beings. And our deepest hunger is spiritual.

In 2000 the *Wall Street Journal* published an article about the construction of bloated homes — houses that fill up their yards to the property lines, that have enough ostentatious touches to scream, "My house is bigger than your house." They are sometimes called McMansions. No society has ever had so many people living like Solomon. An official with one building company said, "We sell what nobody needs."

That's the world in which we live: *we sell what nobody needs.* But the problem of the human heart is: *we need what nobody sells.*

One hundred years ago social critic John Ruskin wrote, "There is no wealth but life—life, including all its powers of love, of joy, and of admiration. That country is richest which nourishes the greatest number of noble and happy human beings; that man is richest who, having perfected the functions of his own life to the utmost, has also the widest influence to help the lives of others."

What If Our Desires Are Telling Us Something?

Maybe our insatiable natures are telling us something important. If we are not completely satisfied with all this world has to offer, perhaps we were made for another world. Maybe our dissatisfaction has within it an echo of God's dissatisfaction with the way things are. Maybe, if we let it, it could sharpen our hunger when we pray, "Your kingdom come, your will be done on earth as it is in heaven."

Materialism is for most of us God's main rival. And it is possible to get increasingly free of it. Sometimes when I'm speaking, I try a little exercise in dethroning the idol. I ask people to take out their wallets. (You can do this right now if you like.) Hold it for a moment. Caress it if they want. Look inside to see if anybody's home.

It looks like a piece of leather. But it's really the temple of the twenty-first century. Most people in our day believe that their ability to experience happiness is directly associated with the contents of this little container. This is where the god Mammon lives. We give this little piece of leather the power to make us feel secure, successful, and valuable.

It is very hard for us to surrender control of this little piece of leather. The real issue: who's in charge? Are you holding it or is it holding you? So as a little baby step of surrender, I ask people to hand it to the person next to them. At this point, the attention level in the room goes way up. And then I announce that we're going to take an offering. And I encourage people to give with the extravagant generosity they have always wanted to exhibit.

Wallets fly back to their owners real fast at this point. I then invite people to declare today "Enough Day." What I have now — my home, my possessions, my lifestyle — is enough. I will seek another and better kind of wealth than terminal acquisition.

Circle the day on your calendar. From this day on, your race with the Joneses is over. *The Joneses win!*

Contentment Can Be Learned

We are called to contentment. Contentment does not come when we acquire enough. It is a product of the way we think.

Snoopy was on his doghouse one Thanksgiving, grumbling in his spirit about being stuck with dog food while all the humans got to be inside with turkey and gravy and cranberries and pumpkin pie. "Of course, it could have been worse," he finally reflected. "I could have been born a turkey."

Saying the phrase "It could be worse" can be a powerful exercise in the development of contentment. I sometimes do a little chant-ing exercise at seminars on this subject. I

> Contentment does not come when we acquire enough. It is a product of the way we think.

tell the audience that when they leave to get into their cars, they will be tempted to think they would be content if they had a nicer, newer, more expensive car. Instead, just for the day, when they get into their cars, they are to say with great passion (then we all chant together), "It could be worse."

I tell them that when they go home to wherever they live, they will be tempted to think they would be content if they had a nicer, newer, more expensive home. Instead, just for the day, when they walk across the threshold, they are to say to themselves (the chants again), "It could be worse."

I tell them that if they are married, they will be tempted to think that they would be more content if they had a nicer, newer, more expensive spouse. Instead, when they wake up the next morning and look into their spouse's face, they are to say with great passion, "It could be worse." (I don't recommend doing this one out loud, but at seminars this is always the most passionate of the chants.)

Contentment, Paul says, is an acquired skill. "I have *learned the secret* of being content." Philip Yancey writes of a spiritual seeker who interrupted his busy, acquisitive life to spend a few days in a monastery. "I hope your stay is a blessed one," said the monk who showed him to his simple cell. "If you need anything, let us know, and we'll teach you how to live without it."

The Station

Robert Hastings takes us on an imaginary train ride that goes something like the following: Tucked away in the recesses of our mind is an idyllic vision. We see ourselves on a long journey that crosses mountains and plains. We are on a train, and out the window is an endless procession of cars motoring down nearby highways, children waving up at us from crossings, cows grazing on distant hillsides, fields of corn and wheat curtseying in the breeze, lakes and rivers, city skylines, and village halls.

But we don't really notice. What we keep thinking about is the final destination. We will arrive at the station to marching bands and waving flags. Once we get there, our dreams will be fulfilled. The jigsaw pieces of our lives will finally be assembled, the picture will finally be complete. In the meantime, we restlessly roam the aisles, checking our watches, ticking off the stops; always waiting, waiting, waiting for the station. Always wishing the train would go faster.

The name of the train is *more*. The name of the station is *satisfaction*.

"When we reach the station, that will be IT!" we cry.

"When I'm eighteen."

"When I buy a new 450SL Mercedes!"

"When I get the next promotion!"

"When I lose enough weight."

"When we get married and have kids in the house."

"When the kids grow up and get out of the house."

"When I have paid off the mortgage."

"When we can afford a second house."

"When we finally retire and all the pressure is off, then I will live happily ever after."

We keep thinking that a train called *more* will get us to a station called *satisfaction*.

What if trying to pursue satisfaction by having more is like trying to run after the horizon? Why would we ever expect more to be enough here if this is not our home?

What if the train is called *contentment*? What if the station is called *heaven*?

What if the *station* is real and is to be the object of our truest and deepest longings? Then we will see God face-to-face. Then our longings for glory, beauty, love, and meaning will be fully realized. Then the restless human race will finally cry out, "Enough!"

And God will say, "More!"

CHAPTER 18

Winning Alone Is Called Losing

Happy is the house that
shelters a friend.
Ralph Waldo Emerson

The football team at Northwest High School in McDermott, Ohio, had a young man named Jake Porter on its roster. Jake has a disorder called chromosomal fragile-x, which means he is cognitively challenged. He will never be Master of the Board.

But Jake loves football. He went out for the team as a freshman and showed so much spirit the coach didn't have the heart to cut him. All the way through high school he came to every practice, he ran through every drill, he dressed in full gear for every game on the schedule knowing that he would never actually get on the field or play a down of real football.

The schedule was winding down to the last game of his senior year. His coach, Dave Frantz, wanted Jake to get in the game, so he explained Jake's situation to the coach of the opposing team. He asked, if the score was lopsided at the end, if it would be okay if they put Jake in for a play. They had practiced all week having Jake take a handoff and touch one knee to the ground so no one would risk hurting him.

The other coach agreed.

Five seconds to go in the game, Jake's team was losing forty-two to nothing. Coach Frantz figured that qualified as lopsided, so he called a time-out. He was going to put Jake in the game.

Suddenly the opposing coach came sprinting across the field. People wondered what was going on. Dave Frantz thought perhaps he was upset; maybe he'd changed his mind. "Do you have concerns about Jake getting in the game?" Dave asked him.

"Yes, I do," he said. "I don't just want him to get in the game; I want him to score." Coach Frantz didn't know what to say. The opposing team's head coach was also the defensive coordinator; a score would mean his defense would lose their shutout. No coach gives up a shutout.

Coach Frantz said, "But we haven't practiced that. We've just done the knee thing."

"You give him the ball. We'll make sure he scores."

Coach Frantz went back to the huddle. He pointed to Jake. "Big Boy, you're going to the house." Jake started jumping up and down. The sheer audacity of the idea caught everyone off guard.

The quarterback called his play, 84-iso, the ball was snapped, and he handed off to Jake. What happened next is an Ohio football legend.

Jake had practiced taking a knee so many times that he started to go down. His knee came within two inches of the ground, and his whole team started yelling at him not to go down.

He took a few steps backward, and his teammates were all pointing toward the end zone.

Dave and the rest of Jake's coaches, yelling on the sidelines, were pointing toward the end zone. The players on the opposing team were pointing toward the end zone. The referees were pointing toward the end zone.

Jake walked slowly toward the line of scrimmage. Twenty-one players parted in front of him as if they were the Red Sea and he was Moses, and then he took off for the Promised Land. Canaan was forty-nine yards away. It took him almost twelve seconds. Everybody on the sidelines was running step-for-step with him.

And Jake Porter scored a touchdown.

The bleachers exploded. Everybody was cheering. Grown men were crying; hardened football warriors were hugging each other. A lot of boys played in that game. When they grow to be old men, they will forget details about most of the games they played in. They won't remember many scores. But not one of them will forget the day Jake Porter scored a touchdown. Jake's touchdown became everybody's touchdown.

Nothing Else Matters without It

The apostle Paul said that without love he was nothing. He contrasted love with spiritual accomplishments: "If I speak in the tongues of men and of angels.... If I ... can fathom all mysteries and all knowledge, and if I have a faith that can move mountains, but have not love, I am nothing.... I gain nothing." The same is true for accomplishments in any arena: If I make a fortune, get the cover of *Time* magazine, and become attractive, comfortable, and secure, but have not love, I have rolled snake eyes. No matter how much I win, if I win it alone, I lose. Love is the ball game.

> *No matter how much I win, if I win it alone, I lose. Love is the ball game.*

In Jesus' parable of the rich fool, we discover that the rich man was alone with his wealth, for when he had a bumper crop and needed to make a decision about what to do with it, he had a discussion with himself, asking, "What shall I do?"

Scholar Kenneth Bailey notes, "One of the striking features of the traditional Middle Easterner is his gregarious nature. Life is lived in tightly knit communities. The leading men of the village still 'sit at the gate' and spend literally years talking to one another. Often there seems to be a subtle pressure not to introduce the information that will settle the question under discussion: 'We have a wonderful discussion going, do not close it!'"

But the man in Jesus' story had no one to talk to: "He thought *to himself*...." Jesus pictured the man utterly alone. His speech was riddled with references only to himself: "What shall *I* do? *I* have no place to store *my* crops.... This is what *I'll* do. *I* will tear down *my* barns and build bigger ones, and there *I* will store all *my* grain and *my* goods. And *I'll* say to *myself....*"

No children ran around his house. No wife advised him; no friends ate and drank with him. He sat and spoke and made merry all alone. And he died alone as well.

To win alone is to lose. Psychologist Philip Zimbardo of Stanford writes:

> I know of no more potent killer than isolation. There is no more destructive influence on physical and mental health than the isolation of you from me and us from them.... The devil's strategy for our times is to trivialize human existence by isolating us from one another while creating the delusion that the reasons are time pressures, work demands and economic uncertainties; by fostering narcissism and the fierce competition to be No. 1.

Of course, we all say that relationships are more important than money. But we constantly cheat relationships for the sake of work or money. There are no TV shows called "Who Wants to Be a Great Friend?" What we have come to call "reality" shows are programs that deliberately pit one person against another. "Reality" means having someone excluded or fired or voted off the show. If we're going to play the game wisely, there are a few relational realities we need to observe.

Give Relationships Top Priority

Max De Pree was talking to his father one day when his father was in his mid-nineties. His father had been the wildly successful CEO of a Fortune 500 company called Herman Miller half a century ago. They were so innovative in design that one of their chairs sits today in the Smithsonian Institute. They created an employee profit-sharing plan decades before its time. He had been deeply involved in church and community life and had lived wisely and well, but he had lived so long that his wife and longtime friends had all passed away. Max asked him how he was doing, and his dad was deeply sad.

"I've lived too long," he told Max. "I've outlived everybody I knew. It's a hard thing to outlive all your peers. I don't have any friends left—they've all died."

"Don't you have anybody?"

"No. Well, I suppose there is one."

Then he told Max about his one friend. There was, in his neighborhood, an eight-year-old boy who lived nearby. The boy had no father, no real male role model in his life. His path home from school took him past the old man's home. A relationship started when one day they nodded at each other as the boy passed. The nods turned into "hellos." And the hellos turned into conversations. After a while, the boy got in the habit of stopping by two or three times a week on his way home.

"What do you do when he comes by?" asked Max, intrigued by the picture of his ninety-six-year-old ex-CEO father hosting a second grader.

We cannot make friendship and love happen. They come, when they come at all, as gifts. But we can make space for them.

Every day, his dad said, he would fix a glass of milk and a plate of cookies, just in case that day would be the day his friend stopped to visit. On those days when he did, Max's dad would bring the snack outside, and they would sit down and eat it together on the stoop, so that everyone in the neighborhood could see and no one would get suspicious about what they were doing. Then the loneliness of a ninety-six-year-old widowed, world-class CEO, and the loneliness of an eight-year-old, fatherless boy connected and melted away.

We cannot make friendship and love happen. They come, when they come at all, as gifts. But we can make space for them. We can work at reestablishing family fun and meaningful rituals. One of my best friends has had a family pizza night tradition on Fridays for almost two decades now. They start with a primal scream—everybody at the table yelling as loud as they can for about ten seconds to expunge all the frustrations of the week. It may sound goofy, but it has built a family memory that will last a lifetime.

We can turn off the TV. We can travel in cars with conversations instead of iPods and headphones. We can figure out how much physical and emotional energy we need to give attention to those we love and then give our leftovers to work instead of the other way around. We can read together. We can begin by simply making the decision that we *will* give relationships top priority.

Help Somebody Else Win

"Do nothing out of selfish ambition or vain conceit.... Look not only to your own interests, but also to the interests of others," Paul wrote. The way the real game is played, our most cherished and meaningful wins come when we are helping somebody else.

When I lived in Los Angeles, the Dodgers acquired a pitcher named Orel Leonard Hersheiser IV. When you want to make a living throwing a baseball past large men with a bat in their hands, you want a name like Tommy Lethal or Joe Widowmaker—something that suggests danger. Orel Leonard Hersheiser IV is not an asset in the name department. To make things worse, he was a skinny, stoop-shouldered, pale-complexioned, mild-mannered figure who did not intimidate anyone. His first few years in professional ball were a struggle at best.

One day when he was having a typically rocky outing, his manager, Tommy Lasorda, came out to the mound. Tommy had an energy for the game that made the Energizer bunny look lazy, and he had an uncanny ability to get other people to believe in themselves. He walked to the mound and changed Orel's life.

"When I look at you, you know what I see? I don't see a skinny, scared, uncertain kid. I see a fighter. I see a man with guts, with some fire in his belly. I see a bulldog. So from now on, when I talk to you, I'm not calling you Orel Leonard Hersheiser IV anymore. From now on, you're Bulldog."

No one had ever looked at Orel Hersheiser and seen a bulldog before. But Tommy Lasorda did. And he wasn't making it up. There was a bulldog inside that skinny young pitcher. He went on to become a perennial All-Star ace of the staff. And the conversation he had with Tommy Lasorda that day became famous.

They called it "The Sermon on the Mound."

In 1989 Bulldog won the Cy Young Award with one of the most dominating seasons a pitcher has displayed in modern times. He set a record for scoreless innings pitched. In the postseason series against the New York Mets, Bulldog pitched the key game against the Mets and their ace, Ron Darling. As soon as I heard the name of the opposing pitcher, I knew Hersheiser would win, because Tommy Lasorda would stand on the steps of the dugout yelling, "Come on, Bulldog." But Davy Johnson, the Mets manager, could only cry out, "Throw strikes, Darling."

Love Is Eternal but Must Be Given Today

The shape of our family life is changing these days. One of my daughters is spending a semester in Europe, another one began her freshman year in college. We have seen this time coming, of course. And I'm glad it is here. I wouldn't want the kids to be living at home when we're in our nineties and they're sixtysomething. But still, moments come that surprise us with the fearful beauty of life and its brevity.

A few days after both the girls had left home, Nancy went grocery shopping. She picked up three potatoes in the produce section, and the thought hit her, *We used to be a five-potato family.* Then Laura went away to school, and we only needed four. Now Mallory has gone, and we're down to three. Soon it will be Johnny's turn, and then we will be back to the two potatoes who started the whole thing. Nancy, who is usually more of a thinker than a feeler, just stood there in the grocery store with three potatoes in her hand and cried.

Then she got a pack of chocolate Ho Hos and ate them and felt much better.

Our potatoes are going away. I am thrilled for the great adventure they're on. Parenting is the one job in which success is measured by making yourself obsolete. And I enjoy the freedom of this new season. But I'll let you in on a little secret. Sometimes, I miss our potatoes.

What I feel for my kids is only a tiny echo of what God feels for every person I see. The homeless man sitting on a corner hoping someone will put a buck in his cup. The arrogant, unethical boss at work. The suicide bomber in Iraq. The extra-grace-required person who hassles everybody in the family.

A while ago, one of my potatoes was snowboarding and sailed sixty feet in the air off a jump and landed on his neck. He wound up with a separated shoulder, mild concussion, bleeding liver, and some lacerations. The story has a happy ending, but when I had raced to the hospital, I remembered something I had read about how certain moments have the power to remind us about how much of our lives are temporary and how the permanence of love is what binds us together. It was written by a man named Wes Seeliger. It is, in its own way, an echo of the wisdom of Paul.

> I have spent long hours in the intensive care waiting room watching with anguished people, listening to urgent questions: Will my husband make it? Will my child walk again? How do you live without your companion of thirty years?
>
> The intensive care waiting room is different from any other place in the world. And the people who wait are different. They can't do enough for each other. No one is rude. The distinctions of race and class melt away. The garbage man loves his wife as much as the university professor loves his, and everyone understands this. Each person pulls for everyone else.
>
> In the intensive care waiting room, the world changes. Vanity and pretense vanish. The universe is focused on the doctor's next report. If only it will show improvement. Everyone knows that loving someone else is what life is all about.
>
> Could we learn to love like that if we realized that every day of life is a day in the waiting room?

CHAPTER 19

BE THE KIND
OF PLAYER
PEOPLE WANT TO
SIT NEXT TO

*But we all hoped,
in whatever way our capacities permitted,
to define and illustrate the worthy life.*
WALLACE STEGNER

The Monopoly Companion warns players about what can sabotage their games. "Mr. Monopoly," who is perhaps a little underchallenged in his day job, has devoted much of his life to discerning the obstacles that keep people from realizing their full Monopoly potential. Most of his tips have to do with the financial bottom line. Know which properties have the highest return on investment (not Boardwalk and Park Place; people don't land on them enough.) Figure out when to stay in jail (when everyone has hotels).

But the number one strategy tip surprised me. It has nothing to do with financial acumen or a sense of timing. It is simply this: *Be the kind of player other people want to sit next to at the game. Be the kind of player other people don't mind losing to.* Monopoly is a game that cannot be won without trades and deals, and that takes cooperation. Mr. Monopoly says that other players don't like to lose to "browbeaters, insulters, know-it-alls, and inconsiderate players." If that's you, other players will shut you out of trades. "I've seen it happen a zillion times at tournaments," says Mr. Monopoly.

People who cling to resentments, people who do not know how to handle disappointment with grace, people with long memories and short "forgivers," people who choke on the words "I'm sorry," people who sulk and pout and whine—even really smart players who do these things—end up losing at the end of the game.

Become the kind of player other people want to sit next to. The Bible's word for this is grace. Play with grace. Cultivate a gracious spirit. The game presents for every player three challenges that must be navigated with grace.

Lose with Grace

Psychologist Henry Cloud does a lot of corporate consulting and sometimes asks executives this question: "When in your business training or education did you ever take a course on how to lose well?" Losing is an inevitable part of life. Losing gives us an invaluable window into the development of our character. How do we do when we're part of a team that makes a decision that we opposed? How do we handle it when a promotion we have applied for goes to somebody else? What do we do when our idea or proposal or invitation for a date gets rejected? To live is to lose. But to lose badly, gracelessly, can be lethal.

A president of an organization has an agenda for change that is dead in the water. No one wants it. But he is stubborn and won't take no for an answer, so he gets malicious compliance instead. People do not resist him openly, but they sabotage his agenda in a thousand quiet, passive, deadly little ways. He loses their respect and their loyalty. He could not stand to lose on his agenda, so instead, he loses what matters far more.

A pastor wants his church to change in ways that the people do not embrace. He wants it to look like *his* ideal of what a church should look like. Mostly this means he wants it to look *big*. But people sense that his desire has more to do with his ego than anything else. So they vote no in a hundred subtle ways. Still, he cannot bring himself to admit the truth. So he preaches angry sermons that chastise them for not following his leadership. He tries to pressure the elders. He threatens, he whines, he manipulates. Eventually the elders ask him to leave the church. Because he cannot lose and learn from his losses, he loses everything.

Sometimes we lose in personal relationships. Samuel and Susanna Wesley (John Wesley's parents) were at evening prayer one night when Susanna did not say "amen" to her husband's prayer for William of Orange, then king of England. He asked her why, and she explained that her sympathies lay with the deposed James II. This turned into a game of "You do what I say," which he could not win. She wrote about what happened next: "He immediately kneeled down and imprecated the divine Vengeance upon himself and all his posterity if ever he touched me more or came into a bed with me before I had begged God's pardon and his for not saying Amen to the prayer for the king." (Typical of a man to think the greatest punishment he can inflict on his wife is depriving her of having sex with him.) The stalemate lasted six months and was broken only when a tragic fire destroyed two-thirds of their home.

> In the long run, true esteem comes only from knowing we can actually handle reality, which means both wins and losses.

When we played games with my grandmother, she was always fun, but she was also on the lookout for grandchildren who would sulk or pout when they lost (generally that was me, although I had a cousin with the same disease). She would always beat them (generally me). I did not like this quality in her at the time, but I understand it better now. My grandmother was trying to teach me about one of the great challenges of life. In the short run, it seems as though you can build up self-esteem in a child by letting the child win. But in the long run, true esteem comes only from knowing we can actually handle reality, which means both wins and losses. Thus, it is very important for a child to lose sometimes.

Losing well is an art that requires all the grace I can muster. It means having the humility to face reality full in the face with no excuses but the confidence not to allow losing to define my identity. It means no excuses, no blaming, no self-pity — but no self-condemnation either. It means acquiring the discernment to know when to quit (e.g., if I'm five feet eight inches and weigh 150 pounds, it's probably time to trade in my dream of becoming an NFL linebacker) and when to persevere. It means learning how to say congratulations. It means learning to let go of an outcome I cannot change but to hold on to the will to live fully and well.

Learn to Win Gracefully

In an era of flamboyant end-zone celebrations and grandiose trash talking, winning gracefully is perhaps harder than losing gracefully. When I win I'm tempted by arrogance, power, insensitivity, gloating, and wanting to relive my successes long after everyone else is bored by them. Graceful winners always remember what it feels like to lose. And they are caught up in something bigger than their own wins and losses.

Maybe that is why the most gracious winner in the history of American politics was one who had experienced much loss. In *Team of Rivals*, Doris Kearns Goodwin tells how Abraham Lincoln placed in his cabinet all his greatest rivals for the presidency. No one had ever done this before; nor has anyone done it since. Cabinet posts are generally rewards for loyalty. When someone asked Lincoln why he would make such an unusual move, his response was that he would never dream of depriving the country of their leadership when it needed them most. But perhaps the best story of his grace in winning involves his relationship with Edwin Stanton.

In 1854 Abraham Lincoln was working as a lawyer in Springfield, Illinois. He was invited to collaborate with one of the most prestigious firms in the country, a firm based in Washington, D.C., on a lawsuit that would be held in Chicago. It was the biggest case by far he had ever been involved in. He devoted an entire summer to research. What he did not know was that the firm had engaged him solely because they needed a local attorney to ingratiate themselves with an Illinois judge.

The star attorney for the high-powered firm was a brilliant legal giant named Edwin Stanton. He could be brusque and condescending; as Frederick Douglass put it, "Politeness was not one of his weaknesses." Lincoln, on the other hand, was keenly aware of his homely appearance and uneducated background. (When a political opponent charged him with being two-faced during a campaign, Lincoln responded: "Really—if I had two faces, do you think I'd be wearing *this* one?")

Stanton quickly decided he had no use for Lincoln. He read none of Lincoln's briefs and answered none of his letters. When Stanton and another partner arrived at Lincoln's hotel for the trial, Lincoln met them and suggested, "Let's go up in a gang" to court.

"Let that fellow go up with his gang," Stanton whispered to his partner, leaving Lincoln to make his way to court alone. Stanton would not confer with him, eat with him, or plot strategy with him. At one point, Lincoln heard Stanton say to his colleague: "Where did that long-armed creature come from, and what can he expect to do in this case?" His snubs grew so severe that when it became clear Lincoln would not be allowed to contribute, he withdrew from the case.

Fast-forward five years. Abraham Lincoln, the ill-dressed, unkempt, long-armed local lawyer is now president of the United States. He's a winner. Edwin Stanton is the outgoing attorney general. His party lost, and losing has not made him any more gracious toward Lincoln: twice in letters to friends he referred to the "imbecility of Lincoln"; in communicating with the Union general George McClellan, he called Lincoln "the original gorilla." Stanton's own partner said there "was probably no man in the country towards whom Lincoln had reason to feel so much personal resentment."

But the gorilla needed someone to run the War Department. The war was going badly, and the Union armies were in shattered disorganization. Lincoln was advised by a number of experts that the man best suited to righting it was Stanton. So, Lincoln said to a mutual acquaintance, "I have made up my mind to sit down on all my pride — it may be a portion of my self-respect — and appoint him to the place." And how Lincoln treated Stanton is Civil War history. When Stanton joined the cabinet, Lincoln trusted in him, confided in him, leaned on him, depended on him. Lincoln and Stanton established the closest daily working relationship Lincoln had with any of his cabinet members. And Stanton responded with unfailing loyalty and affection. A few years into the war, Stanton met his ex-partner George Harding, who praised a recent state paper and suggested that Stanton had been its real author. "Not a word," Stanton said. "Lincoln wrote it — every word of it. No men were ever so deceived about a man as we." Harding later wrote, "Never afterwards would any disparagement of Lincoln be tolerated by Stanton or members of his family."

On the morning of April 14, 1865, Abraham Lincoln died after having been shot the night before at Ford's Theater. The most famous words ever spoken after the death of a president were spoken that morning: "Now he belongs to the ages." The speaker was Edwin Stanton. Robert Todd Lincoln, Abraham Lincoln's son, said that after his father died, he was called on in his room each morning for two weeks by Edwin Stanton who "spent the first ten minutes of his visits weeping without saying a word."

Learn to Forgive Gracefully

When you play the game, you may win or you may lose, but for certain you will be wounded. And to deal with that hurt, you need that greatest kind of grace available: the grace to forgive.

Imagine being assigned to carry a rock the size of a bowling ball around with you all the time. It's heavy and inconvenient, but you can never put it down. It's called a grudge.

We have interesting language surrounding grudges. We talk about them the way we talk about babies: you can hold a grudge, carry a grudge, or bear a grudge. We even talk about nursing a grudge. When you nurse something, you feed it that which will keep it alive and make it grow. Pretty soon it's full grown. Maybe you have two or three.

Funny thing — you would think no one would pick up one of these heavy burdens and carry it around voluntarily. Nobody has ever said, "I can't wait to pick up my grudge this morning and carry it around another day." But people do — every day.

Lamech might be called the patron saint of the grudge. Lamech lived a few generations after Adam and Eve, on the

> To deal with a hurt, you need the greatest kind of grace available: the grace to forgive.

Cain side of the family, and that's part of his story. When Cain killed his brother Abel, we're told God put a mark on him. The mark was a kind of warning. God said that if anyone killed Cain, he would suffer vengeance seven times over. God knows that once the human race gives in to the desire for revenge, it will destroy itself. God was saying that human beings are not to take vengeance into their own hands.

A few generations later, Lamech was born. We are told a couple of things about him. He married two wives — Adah and Zillah. No one had done that before. God's intent was for there to be one husband and one wife — "two shall become one flesh." Lamech introduced polygamy to the human race, with all the hurt and oppression that would create for women.

One day somebody hurt Lamech. We don't know any of the details. It may have been an accident. In any case, it festered in him. The more he thought about it, the madder he got. That's the way bitterness works. He decided to get even.

He picked up a rock. Lamech said to his wives:

> "Adah and Zillah, listen to me;
>   wives of Lamech, hear my words.
> I have killed a man for wounding me,
>   a young man for injuring me.
> If Cain is avenged seven times,
>   then Lamech seventy-seven times."

Lamech had no sense of guilt, no remorse. In his mind, he was absolutely justified. His enemy had it coming. That's the way bitterness works. This is the code of Lamech: you hurt me, I'll hurt you back. Notice the math: seventy-seven times over. A bitter spirit is never satisfied.

Once your mind is focused on payback, you will never reach the point where you say, "Now I've inflicted enough pain on you — I'm peaceful and content."

There are a lot of ways to kill someone. You can do it with harsh words or with gossip or by just withdrawing. Keep doing that day after day, week after week, and over time you will find that where once you had a heart of love toward a spouse, parent, sibling, friend, or business partner, you now have a heart of stone. Not like Lamech, of course. Not yet. But the forces of bitterness, resentment, judgment, and coldness are all at work destroying the capacity to love.

The strange thing is that not only do we carry these rocks around, but we want to. We know we're *supposed* to forgive other people, but forgiving feels as if we would be giving *up* something. One of Lincoln's favorite stories was about a man in his sickbed who had been told by the doctor that he didn't have much time to live. He summoned an old friend named Brown with whom he had quarreled bitterly. They had not spoken for years. The man spoke of how he was going to die soon, of how petty their differences looked in the face of death, and he asked if they might be reconciled. The scene moved everyone in the sickroom to tears. Brown clasped the man's hands and embraced him. Then he turned to walk out of the room, a shattered man. The man in the sickbed, having one final thought, raised himself up on one elbow and spoke a last time: "But see here, Brown; if I recover, the old grudge still stands."

We tell ourselves that we have a *right* to carry a grudge. A study in the *Journal of Adult Development* found that 75 percent of those surveyed believe they have been forgiven by God for past mistakes and wrongdoing, but only 52 percent say they have forgiven others; and even fewer — 43 percent — say they have actively sought forgiveness for harms they have done.

There is another way. Like Lamech, the apostle Peter had been hurt by someone, and the offense had occurred multiple times. He came to Jesus one day and asked, "How many times do I have to forgive this man? Seven times?" He thought seven was extremely generous and expected Jesus to be quite impressed. Thus he was a little deflated when Jesus answered, 'I tell you, not seven times, but seventy-seven times."

> *We tell ourselves that we have a right to carry a grudge.... But there is another way.*

It's clear where Jesus got the number seventy-seven from. He knew the Hebrew Scriptures and chose that number very deliberately. He was reversing the code of Lamech. "You can follow the way of Lamech and carry a grudge or harbor resentment, or you can follow me and offer forgiveness and seek reconciliation. But you cannot do both. You must choose. Peter: put down the stone." "For if you forgive others when they sin against you, your heavenly Father will also forgive you. But if you do not forgive others their sins, your Father will not forgive your sins."

There is only one safe place for grudges, and that place is at the foot of the cross. At the cross, I remember that I too stand in need of forgiveness. At the cross, I remember that for me to expect to receive ultimate forgiveness purchased at the ultimate price from heaven yet withhold it from someone who has hurt me, is the ultimate contradiction.

The cross is where we see what grace looks like at the moment of ultimate loss: a rejected Messiah carrying your loss and mine with inextinguishable grace: "Father, forgive them, for they know not what they are doing." At the cross we learn to lose with grace.

The cross is the place where we see what grace looks like when it wins, for the cross is the victory of grace over sin and death, where "having disarmed the powers and authorities, [Christ] made a public spectacle of them, triumphing over them by the cross." And his victory became good news for Peter who denied him at the cross and for a Roman centurion who helped hang him there. At the cross we learn to win with grace.

The cross is the place where forgiven sinners receive the grace to forgive others. "Christ brought us together through his death on the Cross. The Cross got us to embrace, and that was the end of the hostility."

At the cross we see what grace looks like when it loses, when it wins, when it forgives. And people are still hoping to sit next to someone who looks like that.

TO WIN

CHAPTER 20

COLLECT THE RIGHT TROPHIES

To please God ...
to be a real ingredient
in the divine happiness.

C. S. LEWIS

The movie *Cool Runnings* tells the unlikely story of the Jamaican bobsled team. At one point, the team members are so desperate to receive an Olympic medal that they are convinced that none of their efforts matter if they end up without it. All the learning, joy, growth, and sacrifice they have devoted themselves to are forgotten next to a piece of metal on a ribbon. Their coach is a four-hundred-pound man who won an Olympic medal for bobsledding twenty years earlier and has been a complete loser ever since. He tells them, "If you're not enough before the gold medal, you're not enough with it."

Rewards

Jesus talked a lot about the rewards of following him. But the pursuit of rewards can break us when we go after the wrong kind. C. S. Lewis distinguished between what might be called intrinsic and extrinsic rewards. If I want to marry a woman for her money, that's seeking an extrinsic reward. It is mercenary and selfish and ultimately will be hollow. If I marry her for love, that too is a kind of reward, but it's the one that properly goes with the action. Love always seeks the enjoyment of its object. The musician who masters her instrument to win louder applause than her rivals is mercenary; the one who plays for the joy of music wins a reward that cannot be taken away.

The difference between intrinsic and extrinsic rewards is the difference between loving to learn versus wanting to have a GPA that will impress others. It's working for the joy of the craft versus working for the corner office or the envied title. It's cultivating a friendship with someone because I simply enjoy being with them versus trying to impress them because I think some of their importance or status could rub off on me.

A trophy is not the achievement itself — it's not the learning that we have gained or the muscles that we have trained or the courage we have expended. It's a *symbol* of achievement. It's an external validation of our worth. At best, the trophies in the case are a little reminder, something to make us grateful for the past and motivated for the future. At its worst, the trophy case becomes a shrine, a tool to prop up a false image of ourselves.

Too much of my life has been about collecting trophies. Living for trophies leaves me hollow, empty, depressed, and tired. Trophies bring a momentary pleasure that can be addicting, but the pleasure always wears off. This is why in heaven when images like "crowns" are used, people are constantly casting them at the Lord's feet. When you give glory and praise and honor away, they bring joy; when you hoard them, they tarnish and fade and become a burden.

God has a wonderful sense of humor and often sends people to help us remember that being enough is his department, and no trophies can confer that status. A few years ago I spoke in a conference in Germany and afterward was asked to sign some books. A woman handed me a German translation of one of my books to sign and said to me in thickly accented English, "Danka. This is the best book I ever read."

Germans aren't famous for their sense of humor, but I thought she might be pulling my leg. "No kidding?" I asked her.

"Yah," she said, by way of a ruthlessly honest explanation, "I don't read much."

My Trophies

My dad had dozens of tennis trophies before I even started playing. I won my first trophy when I was ten years old. Nowadays you have to be a veteran by the time you're ten, but forty years ago it was considered young. The trophy was a small wooden pedestal with a little bronze man on the top with his racquet in back-scratching position getting ready to hit a serve. It was magic, a drug. I was a success. It was molten praise, success on a stick. I wanted more.

> *My first trophy was magic, a drug. I was a success. It was molten praise, success on a stick. I wanted more.*

One time when I was thirteen or so, I was at a tournament in Dixon, Illinois. Dixon is a long way from Wimbledon; it was not a prestigious tournament. And I played badly. But my partner and I made it into the finals in doubles. I think we only had to play one match to get there. The guys we played had just started playing the week before. And they both had a broken leg. But I was in the finals. I got a trophy. I didn't have to tell anyone the details when I got home. The trophy let me pretend I was a *winner.*

I used to count my trophies sometimes, mine and my dad's. I wasn't jealous of his, but I did want to get more.

When I was a junior in college, our team qualified for nationals. My partner, Norm, hit his ground strokes with two hands on both his forehand and backhand. He swung a tennis racquet from the heels, like Babe Ruth swung a baseball bat. The other team just tried to avoid being injured. We made it to the quarterfinals where we were thoroughly creamed. But making the quarterfinals was a big deal because it meant we made All-American. I liked how that sounded. It sounded more impressive than it really was. I went to a Division III school—the smallest kind. Among Division II colleges, I never would have qualified for the national tournament. In Division I, I never even would have been able to play on the varsity squad for scores of colleges. I qualified in the lowliest division, with the minimum performance, in doubles not singles.

But I didn't have to say all of that. I could just say the words
All-American.

The problem was, of course, that it didn't tend to come up naturally in conversation. Hardly anybody asked me, "So, have you ever
been an All-American in anything?" (It has taken me about a decade
of writing to figure out how to work it into a book.)

The problem with trophies is that they just sit around collecting
dust. When I was a boy, my mother would dust the trophies. It used
to be part of a woman's job to dust her man's trophies. No more.
When I got married, I put my trophies in a box to bring along. To
my immense surprise, my wife wasn't really interested in dusting my
trophies. Most of them I got rid of. They were cheap enough that they
had started falling apart anyway. A few I have kept for the memory,
but they're not up on a shelf; they're back in the box. "Riches do not
endure forever, and a crown is not secure for all generations."

Other Trophies

When we try to impress people we think are important, we're trophy
collecting. "I am making a deeper impression on the cosmos because
I know this famous person. When the ark sails I will be on it." All
sorts of objects can become trophies: our grades, our houses, people
we have impressed, our bodies, promotions, compliments, clothing
labels. There are now websites where you can go to look for trophy
wives—women whose beauty is a tribute to their husbands' wealth
and power. A trophy is anything you can get other people to look at
that will make them say, "Wow."

Sometimes people imagine that if they went into some more altruistic vocation they would at least have satisfied souls and know
they had pleased God. But every vocation has its own trophies. Some
pastors have trophy churches, tributes to their charisma, troughs at
which the ego feeds. The problem with feeding at a trough, of course,
is that all you ever get is slop.

Glittering Images is Susan Howatch's brilliant novel about a clergyman who has devoted his life to always appearing godly, wise, loving, and charismatic. Meanwhile his soul starves because no one knows him. "They never meet the man I keep hidden. They just meet the man on public display. I call him the glittering image because he looks so good in the mirror. But beyond him ... beyond him lies the angry stranger who appears in the mirror whenever the glittering image goes absent without leave." His ministry becomes his trophy — and his prison.

The Right Stuff

But there is another kind of trophy to collect — the right kind. They are available every day. I don't have to beat anyone else to get one. When Paul wrote to his brothers and sisters at Philippi, he told them that his old crowns — in his case, his religious accomplishments — he now considered rubbish. He was now collecting a new kind of crown: "My brothers and sisters, you whom I love and long for, my joy and crown."

Paul used the same language in writing to his friends in Thessalonica: "For what is our hope, our joy, or the crown in which we will glory in the presence of our Lord Jesus when he comes? Is it not you? Indeed, you are our glory and joy."

Jesus told a story in which two faithful men stood before their returning king and heard him say to each, "Well done, good and faithful servant!" I try to imagine, every once in a while, what it would be like to stand before God and hear those words.

> I try to imagine, every once in a while, what it would be like to stand before God and hear the words, "Well done, good and faithful servant!"

The purpose of life is to make God smile. "May the LORD smile on you." C. S. Lewis said, "To please God ... to be a real ingredient in the divine happiness ... to be loved by God, not merely pitied, but delighted in as an artist delights in his work or a father in a son — it seems impossible, a weight or burden of glory which our thoughts can hardly sustain. But so it is."

Etty Hillesum was a lovely, brilliant, young Dutch Jewish girl living in Amsterdam in the late 1930s. Her burning ambition was to be recognized as a great writer. She was eventually incarcerated by the Nazis. Although she could have gained freedom and recognition, she chose to stay with her people so she could alleviate as much suffering as possible before her own eventual death. Her journals record a remarkable transformation of a woman whose control over her external world shrank to nothingness but whose soul became miraculously liberated from despair and pettiness.

She found herself compelled to pray, "as if my body had been meant and made for the act of kneeling." She found herself so enveloped by God, so "invincible in the profound cheer and tender providence" of her faith, that she helped her fellow prisoners with a boldness that stunned them all. "There are moments," she said, "when I feel like a little bird, tucked away in a great protective hand." She wrote these words in a concentration camp.

Etty's ambition changed. Now it was *to be the thinking heart of the barracks*, to bear witness that goodness and beauty existed even in the hell of the camps. Because the soul is infinite with God, she came to truly believe "nothing can happen to me.... Sometimes when I stand in some corner of the camp, my feet planted on Your earth, my eyes raised toward your heaven, tears run down my face, tears of deep emotion and gratitude."

It was as if the more Etty's outer person was enchained and humiliated, the more her inner self was liberated and made beautiful. She found that "by excluding death from our life we cannot live a full life, and by admitting death into our life we enlarge and enrich it."

Etty spent her last days giving hope and care, "with a kind word for everyone she met on the way." Her final words were written on a postcard and thrown off Wagon No. 12, the railroad car she rode to what she knew would be her death in Auschwitz. "We left camp singing," she wrote. The Nazis took control of her possessions, her mobility, her work, her family, her body, and finally her life, yet she believed that they did not truly take anything at all.

The trophy that matters is not on our shelves or résumés. It is the soul that we become. That is the crown that we will one day cast before God.

CHAPTER 21

THE KING HAS ONE MORE MOVE

One day man's wisdom will come not out of books
but from the presence of the living God,
and our Earth will glow brighter than the sun,
and there will be no more sadness.

FYODOR DOSTOYEVSKY

When I was very small, my grandmother sometimes prayed with me the prayer that for generations adults taught their children to say when they went to bed at night:

> *Now I lay me down to sleep,*
> *I pray the Lord my soul to keep.*
> *If I should die before I wake,*
> *I pray the Lord my soul to take.*

That's a cheery way to send kids off to bed, isn't it? I haven't seen any statistics on it, but I bet the recitations per night of this particular prayer have gone way down over the last fifty years or so. There actually was another verse to this prayer that children would recite. Picture the scene.

> *Child:* Our days begin with trouble here,
> Our life is but a span,
> And cruel death is always near,
> So frail a thing is man.
> *Parent:* Good night, honey. Pleasant dreams.

There was a day, much different than ours, when children by the millions said this prayer. Somebody wanted children to know that the earth is fallen and broken and not home. Life is not permanent. Death is both undesirable and inevitable, and human life hangs by a slender thread. We have a soul and not just a body. God is the kind of person who can be trusted with our eternal destiny. To be clear about who keeps our souls is infinitely important.

> The fate of the soul— to whom we entrust it, where it will go when we finally sleep when the game is at an end —has always been the greatest question.

Bedtimes nowadays tend to run more toward telling the moon goodnight and giving all-around blessings. I'm not advocating a comeback for the old "cruel death is always near" close to the day. But the fate of the soul—to whom we entrust it, where it will go when we finally sleep when the game is at an end— has always been the greatest question. And it's worth being clear on alternative points of view.

Ignore Our Mortality

Ernest Becker wrote a book called *The Denial of Death*. His thesis was that "the idea of death, the fear of it, haunts the human animal like nothing else." He said we arrange our lives around ignoring or avoiding or repressing the most irrefutable fact in the world, which is that we're going to die. The desire to deny death is the reason for our workaholism and approval addictions and obsession with security; it is what he calls "the mainspring of human activity."

The Denial of Death was published to great acclaim in 1974. That year Becker won the Pulitzer prize and became famous. That year he also found out he had cancer, and that year he turned to God. That year he also died.

Life is okay. We sing songs about life, we play a game called Life, we name products after it. We buy "life insurance." But what do you have to do to collect it? Die. It's actually death insurance. We don't call it that; it would be too depressing.

One of our most popular cereals is called Life. Think they will ever try to sell a cereal called Death? "For people who like to wake up real slow." Imagine this conversation:

"What do you want for breakfast?"

"I'll have a bowl of Death. Mikey likes it!"

We don't use the *D* word much.

Joan Mitford wrote in a hilarious and scathing book called *The American Way of Death* how we have tried to leech the presence of death from our everyday lives in every way possible. The largest service provider in the "death care" industry noted in a recent manual: "Certain words and phrases long associated with cemeteries sometimes increase sales resistance because they suggest images of a negative, morbid and depressing nature."

Mitford lists some of the rules for language changes laid down by the industry over the years. The *deceased* is carried in what is to be called a *casket coach*, not a *hearse*. The *loved one* (never *corpse*) is shown in a *reposing room*, not a *showroom*. For many centuries, the dead were buried in places called *graveyards*, but that made death sound so serious. (Why else would they call it a *grave*?) So the nineteenth century saw the advent of the *cemetery*, which comes from the Greek for "sleeping place." But after a while, *cemetery* started sounding too bleak, so now the preferred language is *memorial park*, which is filled with *interment spaces*. *Undertakers* have become *funeral directors*; *funeral parlors* are now *chapels*. The word *death* should be avoided as much as possible even when it seems impossible. For instance, *death certificate* should be referred to as *vital information card*.

If the loved one is cremated, then family members are to be given an urn filled with *cremains*, not *ashes*, although cremation is frowned on by the industry for obvious financial reasons. Embalming and death cosmetology have become huge industries, shielding us from having to see what death does to the body. The president of Dinair Airbrush Systems, which specializes in helping loved ones look good, believes that cremation without viewing would be much less popular "if people didn't look so dead—if they looked more alive." She cited a recent survey that said 75 percent of mortuary customers were unhappy with the appearance of the deceased. It makes you wonder about the 25 percent who were happy with what death had done for the looks of their loved ones.

The cemetery movement began in nineteenth-century America as a response to the gloominess of graveyards. Mount Auburn, the nation's first cemetery, was so beautiful that it was for many years the number one tourist attraction in Boston. When people wanted to create Central Park in New York, they modeled it after Mount Auburn. Their rallying cry was "Why not have it all but without the graves?"

> "It's not that I'm afraid to die. I just don't want to be there when it happens."
> — Woody Allen

We keep trying to have it all but without graves. Woody Allen said, "It's not that I'm afraid to die. I just don't want to be there when it happens." And Freud said that we can never believe in our own death, though of course this did not keep him from dying.

Hide Our Mortality

Dr. Sherwin B. Nuland wrote a bestseller in the nineties called *How We Die*, a book that essayist Joseph Epstein notes is "not excessively loaded with jokes." The answer to his title is that we die "too quickly or all too slowly, drearily, painfully, sloppily, undignifiedly, horrendously, but—and here is the genuinely bad news—inevitably."

Nuland says that early in his career hospitals used to keep what was called a "danger list." When it became clear that someone's life was in peril, when a cure could no longer be reasonably guaranteed, his or her name went on the danger list. This was an indicator that issues deeper than medical ones were in play, and a person's priest or pastor was called. Such a list is no longer kept, writes Nuland, because the appearance of a clergyman may scare the patient by intimating that his or her life is at risk.

Children were once told that babies are brought by the stork, but they were invited to say good-bye at the deathbed of someone they loved. Now they are given lots of biological information about how babies arrive but are told that grandpa is sleeping in a beautiful garden with flowers.

Outsmart Mortality

In Scottsdale, Arizona, there is a company called the Alcor Life Extension Foundation, which is the largest cryonics foundation in the world. For a healthy fee, your body can be frozen at the point of death. Your blood will be filled with anticoagulants, and then you will be stored in a capsule of liquid nitrogen that will freeze you to minus 320 degrees Fahrenheit until you can be reheated later like a pizza and advanced medical technology can cure whatever diseases killed you. Or, if you don't like being cold, a Seattle company called Immortal Genes offers "eternity in a paperweight." For fifty dollars they will preserve your DNA in a little box for the next ten thousand years so you can be cloned whenever it's convenient. They also offer a ten-thousand-year, money-back guarantee, though it's hard to say who will collect it if things go wrong.

We try to outsmart death in more subtle ways: health clubs, skin creams, surgical techniques, new diets, warmer climates, better medications, smarter doctors, and more. Perhaps science will help us live forever, like Gulliver's toothless, hairless, memoryless race of Struldbrugs.

Viktor Frankl refers to an allegorical parable called "Death in Teheran," in which a servant runs to his rich and mighty master in the garden crying out that he has just met Death, who threatened him. He begs his master to give him his fastest horse so he can flee to Teheran. The master consents.

On returning to his house, the master met Death and asked him, "Why did you terrify and threaten my servant?"

"I did not threaten him; I only showed surprise at finding him still here when I planned to meet him tonight in Teheran."

Accept Our Mortality

Some people resign themselves to death. Feminist author Germaine Greer was asked how she would like to be remembered: "Compost," she said. "I'd want people to say she made good compost."

Walt Whitman wrote in *Leaves of Grass*: "I bequeath myself to the dirt to grow from the grass I love / If you want me again, look for me under your bootsoles."

This is the courageous choice of the stoics: "Instead of averting your eyes from the painful events of life, look at them squarely and contemplate them often. By facing the realities of death, loss, and disappointment you free yourself of illusions and false hopes."

Mel Blanc was the voice behind all the cartoon characters in Looney Tunes. At the end of every movie, you would see Porky Pig pop up with the same send-off: "That's all, folks!" Porky was saying, "The show's over. Time to go home." Mel Blanc died a few years ago. Know what his family put on his tombstone? "That's all, folks!"

The Alternative

Still, there is a longing in us that will not go away. The Egyptians built the pyramids. The Greeks put a gold coin under the tongue so the departed could pay the ferryman to cross over the river Styx. And in recent times, Johnny Carson, when asked what he wanted written on his tombstone, said, "I'll be right back."

Philip Yancey writes that our very response to the reality of death is a signal that we were created for something more. One of the indicators of the reality of another world is our attitude toward mortality:

Nature treats death as a normal occurrence, the foundation of the all-important food chain. Only we humans react with shock and elaboration, as though we can't get used to the fact. We dress up our corpses in new clothes, embalm them, and bury them in airtight caskets and concrete vaults to slow natural decay. We act out a stubborn reluctance to yield to this most powerful of life experiences.... In a way unique to our species, we are not fully at home here. As a symptom of that fact, we feel stirrings toward something higher and more lasting.

These are, says Yancey, persistent rumors of another world.

Our longing is not just for a longer life—not even for an indefinite extension, particularly if all such an extension would mean is more of the same. A Christian college in Southern California once sent students door to door to talk with people about spiritual issues. Two of them knocked on one door to find a frenzied mother of three with a vacuum in one hand and a screaming baby in the other arm, food burning on the stove, and a living room so messy it would have qualified as a federal disaster area. "Are you interested in eternal life?" one of the students asked. "Frankly, I don't think I could stand it," said the mom.

We want more than more of the same. We want what's wrong to be put right. We want suffering to stop. We want clean air, meaningful work, honest politicians, clear consciences, ceaseless beauty, instant Internet connections, the end of loneliness and war. We want the whole enchilada. We want heaven. And what we want is in the hands of the Master of the Board and in his final move.

> *We want the whole enchilada. And what we want is in the hands of the Master of the Board and in his final move.*

Reflecting on Our Mortality
Refocuses Hope Where It Belongs

The seventeenth-century Anglican bishop Jeremy Taylor wrote, "Since we stay not here, being people but of a day's abode ... we must look somewhere else for an abiding city, a place in another country to fix our house in, whose walls and foundation is God, where we must find rest, or else be restless for ever."

There is an old story about a florist who mixed up two orders one busy day. One arrangement went to a new business that was opening, and the other went to a family who had a death. The man with the new business came in ticked off: "The flowers that got delivered to my opening day said, "Rest in peace."

The florist said, "You think you're mad; you should have seen the people who just left. A bouquet was delivered to their family's funeral that said, "Good luck in your new location."

Anne Lamott has written, "For the Christian, death is simply a change in address."

Death points beyond itself to eternity. A Christian art form that flourished in the sixteenth and seventeenth centuries featured paintings of common objects of beauty—a vase of flowers, a mandolin, a sideboard with fruit. Tucked somewhere in the painting would be the two reminders of the passing nature of human existence: a skull and an hourglass.

These paintings were called *vanitas art*, from the passage in Ecclesiastes: "Vanity of vanities; all is vanity.... One generation passeth away, and another generation cometh: but the earth abideth for ever." They weren't intended to foster gloom. They were a reminder that every possession and achievement was passing away and therefore not worthy of our hearts or devotion. They were to prepare us for the *ars moriendi*, the art of dying, to be ready for the moment when the soul will meet God and the meaning and value of our lives will be weighed.

Scripture holds out steady hope for those who have been born into God's kingdom:

"Where, O death is your victory? Where, O death, is your sting?"

Precious in the sight of the LORD is the death of his saints.

"Blessed are the dead who die in the Lord."

For this God is our God for ever and ever; he will be our guide even to the end.

All these people were still living by faith when they died.... They admitted that they were aliens and strangers on earth.... They were longing for a better country—a heavenly one.

Ultimate Hope

One day when Jesus' friend Lazarus had died, Jesus showed up at Mary and Martha's request, but he was four days late. Mary said to him the words so many people say when death has ended life: "If only ..." If only Jesus had come sooner, my brother would not have died.

Jesus said to Mary: "I am the resurrection and the life. He who believes in me will live, even though he dies.... Do you believe this?"

It is worth pausing to consider what a staggering claim Jesus makes. Imagine that you had a sick relative and you asked me to come pray but I didn't make it until after your relative had died. You are upset and say, "I wish you would have come and prayed. Maybe God would have heard. Maybe he would have been healed."

Imagine that I said, "Fear not. I am the resurrection and the life. He who believes in me will live, even though he dies. Do you believe this?" You would call the men in little white coats to come and take me away. No human being in their right mind would say that. No religious leader would say that. Buddha never said that. Muhammad never said that. Confucius never said that.

Jesus said that.

Jesus insisted that death itself was not to be allowed to have the last word. He stood at Lazarus's tomb and said, "Take away the stone.... Lazarus, come out!"

And Lazarus did.

One Last Game ...

"[God] has ... set eternity in the hearts of men," the Scriptures say, and my grandmother guarded her heart. She didn't collect many houses or hotels, but that's not why she was going around the board. She honored what mattered most. She left a legacy of life and faith and love that lives on in my brother and sister and me, and in those we love. She always understood one simple truth that a lot of really smart people seem to have trouble remembering: it all goes back in the box.

"There is always that creeping shadow of age which lengthens year by year." These are the last words my grandmother wrote in her little yellow journal. She died of a brain tumor when I was in high school. I never heard her complain. I moved from the room I shared with my brother into her old room, the room where I had so often lost. I finished growing up there. Now I am nearly fifty — middle-aged is the nice term for it; it is accurate as long as I make it to a hundred. Now the shadow creeps for me.

We began this book with the story of a game, and now we will end with one. I mentioned in the introduction that in the Middle Ages the main lesson of this book was taught using the game of chess. "When the board is put away the game is ended, and the men are all put into a bag, and the King lies as often at the bottom as at the top, wherefore the men are then all alike. When Time is put away by Death, the game is at an end ... all are equal in the bag of the earth."

Bishop Kenneth Ulmer is the pastor of a church that meets in Los Angeles at the Forum where the Lakers used to play basketball. He tells the story of two men in a museum who see a painting of a chess game. One character in the painting looked like a man; the other looked very much like the devil. The man was down to his last piece. The title of the painting was *Checkmate*.

One of the two men looking at the painting was an international chess champion. Something about the painting intrigued him. He began to study it. He grew so engrossed that the man with him got a little impatient and asked what he was doing.

> My grandmother always understood one simple truth that a lot of really smart people forget: it all goes back in the box.

The chess champion said, "Something about this painting bothers me. I want to study it awhile. You go ahead and wander around."

When the friend came back after a while, the chess master said, "We must locate the man who painted this piece. We must tell him he must either change the picture or change the title. I have determined there is something wrong with this painting, and I am an international chess champion."

His friend asked, "What's wrong with the painting?"

The man replied, "It's titled *Checkmate*, but the title is wrong. *The king still has one more move.*"

A little boy named David is up against a giant named Goliath. David is so small he can't even wear grown-up armor or hold a grown-up sword. It looks like checkmate. *But the king still has one more move.*

A man named Daniel is thrown into a den of lions because he refuses to stop praying to his God. The lions are hungry, and he's in there all night. At the first light of dawn, King Darius calls down. Daniel tells him the lions have been put on a low-protein diet and he's doing fine. *The king still has one more move.*

A man named Moses convinces a nation of oppressed slaves to run away from the most powerful man on earth. Pharaoh sets out after them. They're standing on the shore, the Red Sea in front of them, the greatest army in the world behind them. The people say to Moses, "What were you thinking?" *But the king still has one more move.*

A man named Jesus goes to Jerusalem. On Good Friday the earthly powers that be tried him and judged him, whipped him and beat him, mocked him and scorned him, hung him on a cross to die, and threw him in a tomb to rot in the way every human body has rotted since death entered this sorry dark world.

They said to everybody, "That's all, folks! Show's over! Time to go home. Checkmate."

But they were wrong.

One day it's all going back in the box. You may have thought in this life that you were Master of the Board. Or you may have played the role of a pawn. Stuff and titles and what passes for good fortune this time around the game board don't really amount to all that much.

But don't despair. Live wisely. *The king still has one more move.*

Sources

Introduction

7: *Anonymous:* From an ancient Latin manuscript called *Innocentium Papam*, quoted in H. J. R. Murray, *A History of Chess*. Northampton, MA: Benjamin Press, 1913, 330, 334.

Chapter 1: *Learn Rule #1*

11: *Epictetus:* Epictetus, *The Art of Living: The Classic Manual on Virtue, Happiness, and Effectiveness*. A new interpretation by Sharon Lebell. New York: HarperCollins, 1994, 105.

14: *Plato:* Daniel Goleman, *Vital Lies, Simple Truths*. New York: Simon & Schuster, 1985, 237.

15: *Seinfeld:* www.seinfeldscripts.com/TheBoyfriend2.htm.

16: *Lamott:* Anne Lamott, *Bird by Bird: Some Instructions on Writing and Life*. New York: Doubleday, 1994, 195.

17: *Talmud:* Benjamin Blech, *The Complete Idiot's Guide to Understanding Judaism*. New York: Alpha Books, 1999, 157.

Chapter 2: *Be Rich toward God*

21: *Wright:* Steven Wright, quoted in Eugene O'Kelly, *Chasing Daylight*. New York: McGraw-Hill, 2006, 19.

21: *Toycen:* Dave Toycen, *The Power of Generosity*. Toronto: HarperCollins, 2004, 1.

25: *By now you may:* Luke 12:16–21. I am indebted to Haddon Robinson for a sermon I heard on the radio long ago for the idea of retelling the story of the "rich fool" in modern terms.

26: *"I hated all the things":* Ecclesiastes 2:18.

26: *Capozzi:* John Capozzi, quoted in Richard Swenson, *The Overload Syndrome*. Colorado Springs: NavPress, 1999, 187.

26: *Rotgrak:* Lisa Rotgrak, *Death Warmed Over: Funeral Food, Rituals and Customs from Around the World*. Berkeley, CA: Ten Speed Press, 7.

27: *"So it is for everyone"*: See Luke 12:21.

29: *"Then I will dwell"*: Exodus 29:45–46.

29: *"He appointed twelve"*: Mark 3:14.

29: *"Anyone who loves me"*: John 14:23 TNIV.

30: *Hybels:* Bill Hybels, *Just Walk Across the Room.* Grand Rapids: Zondervan, 2006, 186–87.

Chapter 3: *Three Ways to Keep Score*

35: *Lamott:* Anne Lamott, *Bird by Bird: Some Instructions on Writing and Life.* New York: Doubleday, 1994, 123.

35: *Roberts:* Robert Roberts, *Taking the Word to Heart.* Grand Rapids: Eerdmans, 1993, 56.

37: *Abel's burnt offering found favor:* See Miroslav Volf, *Exclusion and Embrace: A Theological Exploration of Identity, Otherness, and Reconciliation.* Nashville: Abingdon, 1996, 102.

37: *"Cain was very angry"*: Genesis 4:5.

38: *Rachel and Leah:* See Genesis 29:16 — 30:24.

38: *"When his brothers saw"*: Genesis 37:4.

38: *"Saul has slain his thousands"*: 1 Samuel 18:7.

38: *"You have plenty"*: Luke 12:19.

39: *Festinger:* Heard in graduate school.

41: *Vidal:* Gore Vidal, quoted in William B. Irvine, *On Desire: Why We Want What We Want.* Cambridge: Oxford University Press, 2005, 37.

42: *Griffiths:* Jay Griffiths, *A Sideways Look at Time.* New York: Tarcher, 2004, 38.

42: *Kushner:* Harold Kushner. Publication information unknown.

45: *"Your attitude should be"*: Philippians 2:5–7.

45: *"Therefore God exalted him"*: Philippians 2:9, italics mine.

Chapter 4: *Master the Inner Game*

47: *The Inner Game of Tennis:* Tim Gallwey, *The Inner Game of Tennis.* New York: Random House, 1974, 13.

47: *"We do not lose heart"*: 2 Corinthians 4:16.

49: *"Do not consider"*: 1 Samuel 16:7.

49: *"It doesn't bother me much"*: Loose summary of thoughts expressed in such passages as 1 Corinthians 15 and Philippians 1.

50: *"The hardest thing to bear"*: Jean-Louis Servan-Schreiber, *The Art of Time.* New York: Marlowe & Company, 2000, 7.

50: Oscar Wilde, *The Picture of Dorian Gray.* Edited by Michael Patrick Gillespie. New York: W. W. Norton, 2006.

51: *"Dear friends"*: 1 John 3:2.
52: *"Who shall separate us"*: Romans 8:35.

Chapter 5: *Untie Your Ropes*

53: *Thoreau:* Henry David Thoreau, *The Portable Thoreau.* New York: Viking Press, 1947, 278.
55: *"Therefore, since"*: Hebrews 12:1.
55: *"Who am I"*: See Exodus 3:11; 4:1, 10.
55: *"Why have you come"*: 1 Samuel 17:28.
57: *"I just bought a field"*: See Luke 14:15–24.
58: *"Go, sell all you have"*: See Matthew 19:16–22.

Chapter 6: *Resign as Master of the Board*

59: *L'Engle:* Madeleine L'Engle, quoted in John Eldridge, *The Journey of Desire.* Nashville: Thomas Nelson, 2000, 89.
59: *Cicero:* Marcus Tullius Cicero in a letter to Demetrius Brutus, quoted in Cicero's *Epistulae ad Familiares,* Book 9.
60: *"And it came to pass"*: Luke 2:1 KJV.
60: *Wright:* Tom Wright, *The Lord and His Prayer.* Grand Rapids: Eerdmans, 1996, 78.
60: *Notice the result:* See Micah 5:2.
61: *Becker:* Ernest Becker, *The Denial of Death.* New York: Free Press, 1974, 55.
61: *"He controls his life"*: Ibid.
61: *Yertle the Turtle:* Dr. Seuss, *Yertle the Turtle and Other Stories.* New York: Random House, 1958.
62: *De Pree:* Max De Pree, *Dear Zoe: Letters to My Miracle Grandchild.* New York: HarperCollins, 1999, 43.
62: *"When you eat"*: Deuteronomy 8:12–18.
63: *"Many are the plans"*: Proverbs 19:21 TNIV.
63: *"I am of the nature"*: Thich Nhat Hanh, *The Plum Village Chanting Book.* Berkeley, CA: Parallax Press, 1991, n.p.
64: *"A person may yield"*: Arnold Heinrich, *Discipleship.* Farmington, PA: Plough, 1994, 77.
64: *One man was not grateful:* Peter F. Drucker, "The Discipline of Innovation," *Harvard Business Review,* August 2002, 6.
66: *Epictetus:* Epictetus, *The Art of Living: The Classic Manual on Virtue, Happiness, and Effectiveness.* A new interpretation by Sharon Lebell. New York: HarperCollins, 1994, 3.
67: *"Simply let your 'Yes' "*: Matthew 5:37.

67: *Didion:* Joan Didion, *The Year of Magical Thinking*. New York: Knopf, 2005, 98.

68: *"No eye is on the sparrow":* Ibid., 227.

68: *"Don't be afraid":* Genesis 50:18–20.

Chapter 7: No One Else Can Take Your Turn

71: *Rabbinic saying:* Quoted in Jacob Needleman, *Why Can't We Be Good?* New York: Penguin Group, 2007, 12.

71: *Suits:* See also Bernard Suits, *The Grasshopper: Games, Life and Utopia*. Toronto: University of Toronto Press, 1978.

73: *"But Daniel determined":* Daniel 1:8 MSG, italics mine.

74: *"Now God had caused":* Daniel 1:9, italics mine.

76: *"Then God said":* Genesis 1:26, my paraphrase.

77: *Human beings are even more:* James Loeher, *Stress for Success*. New York: Times Business, 1997, 61ff.

78: *In concentration camps:* Julius Segal, *Winning Life's Toughest Battles: Roots of Human Resistance*. New York: McGraw-Hill, 1986, 42.

78: *Epictetus:* Epictetus, *The Art of Living: The Classic Manual on Virtue, Happiness, and Effectiveness*. A new interpretation by Sharon Lebell. New York: HarperCollins, 1994, 3.

78: *David Rabin was a professor:* Segal, *Winning Life's Toughest Battles*, 46ff.

79: *"Sickness may challenge":* Ibid., 16.

80: *Baker:* Dan Baker and Cameron Stauth, *What Happy People Know*. Emmaus, PA: Rodale, 2003, 176.

80: *Frankl:* Quoted in Stephen R. Covey, *The Seven Habits of Highly Effective People*. NewYork: Simon & Schuster, 1989, 69.

81: *One writer puts it:* Ibid.

81: *Dare to be a Daniel:* Words and music by Philip P. Bliss, 1873.

Chapter 8: Remember Your Stuff Isn't Yours

83: *Socrates:* Socrates, *The Trial and Death of Socrates*. Translated by G. M. A. Grube. Indianapolis: Hackett, 1975, 30 a-b.

83: *It's larger than the music industry:* John de Graaf et al., *Affluenza: The All-Consuming Epidemic*. San Francisco: Berrett-Koehler Publishers, 2001, 37.

83: *Pearsall:* Paul Pearsall, *Super Joy: Learning to Celebrate Everyday Life*. New York: Doubleday, 1988, 139.

85: *"Do not store up":* Matthew 6:19–21.

85: *This is Motel 6:* This analogy was prompted by a similar analogy of staying at a motel in Randy Alcorn, *The Treasure Principle*. Sisters, OR: Multnomah, 2001, chap. 3.

86: *"The earth is the* LORD'*s"*: Psalm 24:1.

86: *"Remember the* LORD*"*: Deuteronomy 8:18.

86: *"The silver is mine"*: Haggai 2:8.

86: *"But who am I"*: 1 Chronicles 29:14.

87: *"There were no needy"*: Acts 4:34.

87: *Alcorn:* Alcorn, *Treasure Principle*, 47.

88: *"Those who want"*: 1 Timothy 6:9 TNIV.

88: *By the mid-1970s:* Alain de Botton, *Status Anxiety.* New York: Pantheon Books, 2004, 21.

89: *"We brought nothing"*: 1 Timothy 6:7.

89: *"Naked I came"*: Job 1:21.

89: *Calls such emotion "elevation":* As told in Martin Seligman, *Authentic Happiness.* New York: Free Press, 2002, 8.

90: *"We were going home"*: Ibid.

90: *Seligman:* Ibid., 9.

91: *"Shall I give"*: See 2 Samuel 24:24; 1 Chronicles 21:24.

91: *Volf:* Miroslav Volf, *Free of Charge.* Grand Rapids: Zondervan, 2005, 109.

92: *"Though he was rich"*: 2 Corinthians 8:9.

92: *He found that whether:* See Philippians 4:12.

94: *Epstein:* Cited in John Maxwell, *Today Matters.* New York: Warner Books, 2004, 217ff.

94: *"He fired his top executives"*: Ibid., 221.

Chapter 9: *Prevent Regret*

97: *Tolstoy:* Leo Tolstoy, from *The Death of Ivan Ilyitch* in *The Works of Leo Tolstoi,* vol. I. New York: Walter J. Black, 1928, 160.

97: *Carlyle:* Thomas Carlyle, quoted in Alain de Botton, *Status Anxiety.* New York: Pantheon Books, 2004, 200.

99: *Weil:* Simone Weil, quoted in Jean-Louis Servan-Schreiber, *The Art of Time.* New York: Avalon, 2000, 8.

99: *Johnson:* Dr. Timothy Johnson, *Finding God in the Questions: A Personal Journey.* Downers Grove, IL: InterVarsity Press, 2004, 185.

100: *"Do Your Commitments . . . ?":* Donald Sull and Dominic Houlder, "Do Your Commitments Match Your Convictions?" *Harvard Business Review,* January 2005, 82–89.

100: *"No one serving"*: 2 Timothy 2:4.

101: *Husbands and wives spend:* Robert Putnam, *Bowling Alone.* New York: Simon & Schuster, 2000, see chap. 13.

101: *Parents spend: All-Consuming Passion: Waking Up from the American Dream.* New Road Map Foundation. www.scn.org/earth/lightly/karvsacp.htm. Accessed March 20, 2007.

102: *Morley:* Patrick Morley, *The Man in the Mirror.* Grand Rapids: Zondervan, 1997, 111.

102: *"Why do they not teach you":* Pat Conroy, *My Losing Season.* New York: Dial Press, 2002, 324.

102: *Irion:* Publication information unknown.

103: *Muggeridge:* Malcolm Muggeridge, quoted in Stephen R. Covey, *The Seven Habits of Highly Effective People.* New York: Simon & Schuster, 1989, 115.

104: *"What do people get":* See Ecclesiastes 1:3–4, 8, 14 NLT.

104: *Buechner:* Frederick Buechner, *Beyond Words.* San Francisco: HarperSanFrancisco, 2004, 162.

105: *Lynch:* Thomas Lynch, *The Undertaking: Life Studies from the Dismal Trade.* New York: Penguin, 1997.

105: *"What I was trying":* Ibid., 7.

Chapter 10: *Play by the Rules*

111: *MacDonald:* George MacDonald, *Knowing the Heart of God.* Minneapolis: Bethany House, 1990, 116.

111: *"10. WASTING TIME":* Eric Bronson, ed., *Baseball and Philosophy.* Chicago: Open Court, 2004, 73.

112: *"Yes, son":* Cited in Lewis Smedes, *A Pretty Good Person.* Grand Rapids: Eerdmans, 1990, 78–79.

112: *"Save me, O LORD":* Psalm 120:2.

113: *"Each of you must":* Ephesians 4:25.

113: *"Do not lie":* Colossians 3:9.

113: *"The LORD abhors":* Proverbs 11:1.

114: *Seligman:* Martin Seligman, *Authentic Happiness.* New York: Free Press, 2002, 8.

117: *"Blessed are the poor":* Matthew 5:1–12.

117: *"You are the salt":* Matthew 5:13–14.

118: *"If your right eye":* Matthew 5:29–30.

119: *This self-serving bias:* William B. Irvine, *On Desire: Why We Want What We Want.* Cambridge: Oxford University Press, 2005, 35. Research other than the sociologist study cited in this section is from Mark McMinn, *Why Sin Matters.* Wheaton: Tyndale, 2004, chaps. 5–7.

120: *National surveys show:* Gilbert Brim, *Ambition.* New York: HarperCollins, 1992, 78.

120: *"Do not think of yourself":* Romans 12:3.

120: *U.S. News and World Report survey:* Cited in Tim Alan Gardner, *The Naked Soul: God's Amazing, Everyday Solution to Loneliness.* Colorado Springs: WaterBrook, 2004.

122: *"The most important part":* James Stalker, *The Life of Christ.* 1880, reprint Grand Rapids: Zondervan, 1984, chap. V.109.

Chapter 11: *Fill Each Square with What Matters Most*

123: *Smedes:* Lewis Smedes, *How Can It Be All Right When Everything Is All Wrong?* New York: HarperCollins, 1982, 147–48.

124: *Swenson:* Richard A. Swenson, *The Overload Syndrome: Learning to Live within Your Limits.* Colorado Springs: NavPress, 1999, 173.

125: *You will spend:* James Gleick, *Faster: The Acceleration of Just About Everything.* New York: Vintage Books, 2000, 229.

125: *Franklin:* Cited in Carl Honore, *In Praise of Slowness.* San Francisco: HarperSanFrancisco, 2004, 188.

125: *Ryan:* John de Graaf et al., *Affluenza: The All-Consuming Epidemic.* San Francisco: Berrett-Koehler Publishers, 2001, 38.

125: *Wright:* Steve Wright, quoted in Gleick, *Faster,* 136.

126: *Shor:* Juliet Shor, *The Overworked American.* New York: Basic Books, 1992, 88–89.

126: *And you will spend four minutes:* Gleick, *Faster,* 128ff.

127: *One medical ad targeted:* Ibid., 11.

127: *"Seek first the kingdom":* Matthew 6:33 NKJV.

128: *"Very early in the morning":* Mark 1:35.

130: *"I want to be sure he knows":* Herb Gardner, *Herb Gardner: The Collected Plays.* New York: Applause, 2000, 58–59.

131: *"Devote yourself":* 1 Timothy 4:13–14, italics mine.

131: *"I have told you":* John 15:11.

132: *"Rejoice in the Lord":* Philippians 4:4.

132: *There was a rabbinic tradition:* From a sermon by Kim Engelmann at Menlo Park Presbyterian Church, November 6, 2005.

132: *Siegel:* Bernie Siegel, quoted in John Maxwell, *Today Matters.* New York: Warner Books, 2004, 92.

132: *"Squeeze you into its own mold":* Romans 12:2 Phillips.

133: *Harris:* Sydney J. Harris, quoted in Peter McWilliams, *Do It!* Allen Park, MI: Prelude, 1991, 1.

133: *"Who of you by worrying":* Matthew 6:27.

136: *Smedes:* Smedes, *How Can It Be All Right. . . ?* 148.

Chapter 12: *Roll the Dice*

137: *Buechner:* Frederick Buechner, *Beyond Words.* San Francisco: HarperSanFrancisco, 2004, 49.

137: *Lauden:* Larry Lauden, *Danger Ahead.* New York: John Wiley, 1997, 40.

139: *"A man can't just sit there"*: Cited by Wendy Northcutt, *The Darwin Awards.* New York: Dutton, 2000, 280–81.

140: *"I do not have time"*: Hebrews 11:32–38.

141: *"[God] will not let"*: 1 Corinthians 10:13.

142: *"Have I not commanded"*: Joshua 1:9.

142: *"The Lord is with you"*: Judges 6:12.

144: *"When they saw"*: Acts 4:13.

Chapter 13: *Play with Gratitude*

147: *Goldstein:* Shanti Goldstein, *I Am My Own Best Casual Acquaintance.* Chicago: Contemporary Books, 1993, 16.

149: *"The ground of a certain"*: Luke 12:16.

150: *Gregory:* Joel Gregory, quoted in *Fresh Illustrations for Preaching and Teaching,* ed. Edward K. Rowell. Grand Rapids: Baker, 2000, 206.

150: *Baker:* Dan Baker and Cameron Stauth, *What Happy People Know.* Emmaus, PA: Rodale, 2003, 10.

151: *Dodson:* James Dodson, *Final Rounds.* New York: Bantam, 1996, 199.

154: *Emmons and McCullough:* Cited in Martin Seligman, *Authentic Happiness.* New York: Free Press, 2002, 72.

155: *Seligman:* Ibid., 74.

156: *C. S. Lewis:* Cited in Lewis Smedes, *A Pretty Good Person.* Grand Rapids: Eerdmans, 1990, 19.

156: *"Wake up, O sleeper"*: Ephesians 5:14.

Chapter 14: *Find Your Mission*

157: *Shaw:* George Bernard Shaw, *Man and Superman.* New York: Airmont Publishing, 1965, 27.

158: *Johnny the bagger:* Ken Blanchard first told me this story in a phone conversation; it's now in a book he and Barbara Glanz coauthored called *The Simple Truths of Service.* Colorado Springs: Simple Truths Press, 2005.

160: *"Each one should retain"*: 1 Corinthians 7:17.

161: *Bell:* Rob Bell, *Velvet Elvis: Repainting the Christian Faith.* Grand Rapids: Zondervan, 2005, 167.

161: *"You are the salt"*: Matthew 5:13.

162: *"What is that"*: Exodus 4:2.

162: *Seligman:* Martin Seligman, *Authentic Happiness.* New York: Free Press, 2002, chap. 14.

162: *Seligman:* Ibid.

163: *Ellis:* Joseph Ellis, *His Excellency: George Washington.* New York: Knopf, 2004, 43.

164: *Buechner:* Frederick Buechner, *Beyond Words.* San Francisco: HarperSanFrancisco: 2004, 405–6.

Chapter 15: *Beware the Shadow Mission*

169: *King:* Martin Luther King Jr., quoted in John Winokur, ed., *In Passing.* Seattle: Sasquatch, 2005, 57.

170: *"Confess your sins":* James 5:16.

171: *The rich fool:* See Luke 12:18–20.

172: *"By flagons"* and *"when the king":* Esther 1: 8, 10 NRSV.

172: *"In order to display":* Esther 1:11.

173: *"Then the king":* Esther 1:12.

173: *"Lovely in form":* Esther 2:7.

174: *"Pay him honor":* Esther 3:2.

175: *"Who knows":* Esther 4:14.

176: *"And if I perish":* Esther 4:16.

176: *"What is your petition?"* Esther 5:6.

177: *"His vast wealth":* Esther 5:11, 13.

177: *"This suggestion delighted Haman":* Esther 5:14.

177: *"What should be done":* Esther 6:6.

177: *"This is what is done":* Esther 6:9.

178: *"Where is the man":* Esther 7:5.

178: *"The adversary":* Esther 7:6.

178: *"Esther appointed":* Esther 8:2.

178: *"Write another decree":* Esther 8:8.

178: *"Many people":* Esther 8:17.

179: *"In every way":* Hebrews 4:15.

179: *Bruce:* F. F. Bruce, *The Epistle to the Hebrews.* Grand Rapids: Eerdmans, 1964, 53.

179: *"His angels":* Matthew 4:6, 9.

179: *"Get behind me":* Mark 8:33.

180: *"Take this cup":* Mark 14:36.

180: *"My God, my God":* Mark 15:34.

Chapter 16: *Two Cheers for Competition*

181: *Allen:* Woody Allen, quoted in Jean-Louis Servan-Schreiber, *The Art of Time.* New York: Marlowe & Company, 2000, 62.

181: *Hillenbrand:* Laura Hillenbrand, *Seabiscuit.* New York: Ballantine, 2001, 255ff.

183: *"One thing I do":* Philippians 3:13–14.

183: *"I have fought":* 2 Timothy 4:7.

183: *"Do you not know"*: 1 Corinthians 9:24.

183: *MacDonald*: Gordon MacDonald, *A Resilient Life: You Can Move Ahead No Matter What*. Nashville: Thomas Nelson, 2004, 2.

184: *Peterson*: Eugene Peterson, *A Long Obedience in the Same Direction*. Downers Grove, Ill.: InterVarsity Press, 1980.

185: *"Everyone who competes"*: 1 Corinthians 9:25–26.

185: *"The world was not worthy"*: Hebrews 11:38–39.

185: *"Since we are surrounded"*: Hebrews 12:1.

186: *"Knit you together"*: See Psalm 139:13.

Chapter 17: *More Will Never Be Enough*

189: *Dostoyevsky*: Fyodor Dostoyevsky, *The Brothers Karamazov*, quoted in Philip Harnden, *Traveling Light*. Woodstock, VT: Skylight Paths, 2003, 20.

190: *Drosnin*: Michael Drosnin, *Citizen Hughes*. New York: Bantam Books, 1985, 49ff.

192: *"I thought in my heart"*: Ecclesiastes 2:1.

192: *"I denied myself nothing"*: Ecclesiastes 2:10.

192: *"I turned my head"*: Ecclesiastes 4:8 MSG.

192: *"All man's efforts"*: Ecclesiastes 6:7.

192: *"Whoever loves money"*: Ecclesiastes 5:10.

193: *Prager*: Dennis Prager, *Happiness Is a Serious Problem: A Human Nature Repair Manual*. New York: HarperCollins, 1998, 115.

194: *Easterbrook*: Greg Easterbrook, *The Progress Paradox*. New York: Random House, 2003, 9.

194: *Chart*: Ibid, xviii.

194: *Gallup poll*: Cited in Dan Baker and Cameron Stauth, *What Happy People Know*. Emmaus, PA: Rodale, 2003, 45.

195: Janoff-Bulman: P. Brickman, D. Coates, and R. Janoff-Bulman, "Lottery Winners and Accident Victims: Is Happiness Relative?" *Journal of Personality and Social Psychology* 36 (1978), 917–27.

195: *Diener*: Cited in Martin Seligman, *Authentic Happiness*. New York: Free Press, 2002, 186.

196: *The Dutch have never been quite so free*: John Train, *Famous Financial Fiascos*. New York: Fraser, 1995, 9.

196: *"Which is idolatry"*: Colossians 3:5.

196: *Marshall*: I. Howard Marshall, *The Gospel of Luke: A Commentary on the Greek Text*. New International Greek Testament Commentary. Grand Rapids: Eerdmans, 1978, 521.

197: *Ruskin*: John Ruskin, quoted in Alain de Botton, *Status Anxiety*. New York: Pantheon Books, 2004, 199.

199: *"I have learned"*: Philippians 4:12, italics mine.

199: *Yancey:* Philip Yancey, *Prayer: Does It Make Any Difference?* Grand Rapids: Zondervan, 2006, 54.

199: *Hastings:* Adapted from Robert J. Hastings, "The Station," www.storybin. com/wisdom/wisdom104.shtml. Accessed March 19, 2007.

Chapter 18: *Winning Alone Is Called Losing*

201: *Emerson:* Ralph Waldo Emerson, from "Friendship" in *Collected Works: Essays,* First Series (1841).

201: *The football team:* James Walker in the *Herald-Dispatch* newspaper in Huntington, West Virginia, November 10, 2002. See various websites, including www.bridges4kids.org/articles/1-03/Herald11-10-02.html and other websites. Accessed January 22, 2007.

203: *"If I speak":* 1 Corinthians 13:1–3.

203: *Bailey:* Kenneth E. Bailey, *Poet and Peasant.* Grand Rapids: Eerdmans, 1992, 65.

203: *"He thought to himself":* Luke 12:17–19, italics mine.

204: *Zimbardo:* Philip Zimbardo, quoted in Chuck Swindoll, *The Seasons of Life.* Portland, OR: Multnomah,1983, 337.

204: *Max De Pree:* Personal communication.

206: *"Do nothing out of selfish":* Philippians 2:3–4.

208: *Seeliger:* Wes Seeliger, quoted in *Fresh Illustrations for Preaching and Teaching,* ed. Edward K. Rowell. Grand Rapids: Baker, 2000, 141.

Chapter 19: *Be the Kind of Player People Want to Sit Next To*

209: *Stegner:* Wallace Stegner, *Crossing to Safety.* New York: Penguin Books, 1987, 12.

209: *The Monopoly Companion:* Philip Orbanes, *The Monopoly Companion.* New York: Adams Media, 1999, 12.

210: *Henry Cloud:* Personal communication.

211: *Fire destroyed two-thirds of their home:* Cited in Richard Foster, *Streams of Living Water.* San Francisco: HarperSanFrancisco, 1998, 286.

212: *Goodwin:* Doris Kearns Goodwin, *Team of Rivals: The Political Genius of Abraham Lincoln.* 1990, reprint New York: Simon & Schuster, 2006.

212: *In 1854 Abraham Lincoln:* Most of the following story is from William Lee Miller, *Lincoln's Virtues: An Ethical Biography.* New York: Knopf, 2002, 423ff.

215: *"Adah and Zillah":* Genesis 4:23–24.

216: *Journal of Adult Development:* Reported in *Christian Century,* January 2–9, 2002, 15.

217: *"How many times":* See Matthew 18:21–22.

217: *"For if you forgive others":* Matthew 6:14–15 TNIV.

217: *"Father, forgive them"*: Luke 23:34.

217: *"Having disarmed the powers"*: Colossians 2:15.

218: *"Christ brought us together"*: Ephesians 2:16 MSG.

Chapter 20: **Collect the Right Trophies**

221: *Lewis*: C. S. Lewis, *The Weight of Glory*. 1949, reprint New York: HarperCollins, 2003, 4.

221: *"Riches do not endure"*: Proverbs 27:24.

224: *"I am making"*: Ernest Becker, *The Denial of Death*. New York: Free Press, 1974, 148.

225: *Howatch*: Susan Howatch, *Glittering Images*. New York: Random House, 1986, 209.

225: *"My brothers and sisters"*: Philippians 4:1 TNIV.

225: *"For what is our hope"*: 1 Thessalonians 2:19–20 TNIV.

225: *"Well done"*: Matthew 25:21, 23.

225: *"May the LORD smile"*: Numbers 6:25 NLT.

225: *Lewis*: Lewis, *Weight of Glory*, 13.

226: *Hillesum*: Etty Hillesum, journal entry at Auschwitz, quoted in Susan Bergman, ed., *Martyrs*. San Francisco: HarperSanFrancisco, 1996, 6.

Chapter 21: **The King Has One More Move**

229: *Dostoyevsky*: Fyodor Dostoyevsky, *The Gospel in Dostoyevsky*. Farmington, PA: Plough House Publishing, 1988, 233.

230: *Becker*: Ernest Becker, *The Denial of Death*. New York: Free Press, 1974, ix.

231: *Mitford*: Joan Mitford, *The American Way of Death*. New York: Random House, 1996, 194.

232: *The president of Dinair Airbrush Systems*: Cited in ibid., 10.

232: *Nuland*: Sherwin B. Nuland, *How We Die*. New York: Vintage Books, 1993.

232: *Epstein*: Joseph Epstein, *Narcissus Leaves the Pool*. New York: Houghton Mifflin, 1999, 18.

233: *In Scottsdale, Arizona*: Jay Griffith, *A Sideways Look at Time*. New York: Tarcher, 2004, 321.

233: *Frankl*: Viktor Frankl, *Man in Search of Meaning*. New York: Simon & Schuster, 1984, 77.

234: *Greer*: http://www.brainyquote.com/quotes/authors/g/germaine_greer.html. Accessed March 20, 2007.

234: *Whitman*: Quoted in ibid., 325.

234: *"Instead of Averting"*: Epictetus, *The Art of Living: The Classic Manual on Virtue, Happiness, and Effectiveness*. A new interpretation by Sharon Lebell. New York: HarperCollins, 1994, 28.

234: *Yancey:* Philip Yancey, *Rumors of Another World: What on Earth Are We Missing?* Grand Rapids: Zondervan, 2003, 38–39.

236: *Taylor:* Jeremy Taylor, *Holy Living and Holy Dying.* 1651, reprint New York: Oxford University Press, 1989, 276.

236: *"Vanity of vanities":* Ecclesiastes 1:2, 4 KJV.

237: *"Where, O death":* 1 Corinthians 15:55.

237: *"Precious in the sight":* Psalm 116:15.

237: *"Blessed are the dead":* Revelation 14:13.

237: *"For this God is our God":* Psalm 48:14.

237: *"All these people":* Hebrews 11:13–16.

237: *"I am the resurrection":* John 11:25–26.

238: *"[God] has . . . set eternity":* Ecclesiastes 3:11.

238: *"When the board is put away":* Fifteenth-century manuscript, quoted by H. J. R. Murray, *A History of Chess.* Northampton, MA: Benjamin Press, 1913, 550.

238: *Ulmer:* Heard in a sermon.

BIBLE TRANSLATIONS

Scripture quotations marked KJV are taken from the King James Version of the Bible.

Scripture quotations marked MSG are taken from THE MESSAGE. Copyright © by Eugene H. Peterson 1993, 1994, 1995, 1996, 2000, 2001, 2002. Used by permission of NavPress Publishing Group.

Scripture quotations marked NKJV are taken from the New King James Version. Copyright © 1982 by Thomas Nelson, Inc. Used by permission. All rights reserved.

Scripture quotations marked NLT are taken from the *Holy Bible, New Living Translation*, copyright © 1996. Used by permission of Tyndale House Publishers, Inc., Wheaton, IL 60189 USA. All rights reserved.

Scripture quotations marked NRSV are from the *New Revised Standard Version of the Bible*, copyrighted 1989 by the Division of Christian Education of the National Council of Churches of Christ in the United States of America, and are used by permission. All rights reserved.

Scripture quotations marked Phillips are taken from The New Testament in Modern English, revised edition — J. B. Phillips, translator. © J. B. Phillips 1958, 1960, 1972. Used by permission of Macmillan Publishing Co., Inc.

Scripture quotations marked TNIV are taken from the *Holy Bible, Today's New International Version*™. TNIV®. Copyright 2001, 2005 by International Bible Society. Used by permission of Zondervan. All rights reserved.

WILLOW

Willow Creek Association

Vision, Training, Resources for Prevailing Churches

This resource was created to serve you and to help you build a local church that prevails. It is just one of many ministry tools published by the Willow Creek Association.

The Willow Creek Association (WCA) was created in 1992 to serve a rapidly growing number of churches from across the denominational spectrum that are committed to helping unchurched people become fully devoted followers of Christ. Membership in the WCA now numbers over 12,000 Member Churches worldwide from more than ninety denominations.

The Willow Creek Association links like-minded Christian leaders with each other and with strategic vision, training and resources in order to help them build prevailing churches designed to reach their redemptive potential.

For specific information about WCA conferences, resources, membership and other ministry services contact:

Willow Creek Association
P.O. Box 3188
Barrington, IL 60011-3188
Phone: 847.570.9812
Fax: 847.765.5046
www.willowcreek.com